Praise for *"Love's Young Dream":*

"The letters collected here shed light on a number of interconnected families of Middle Tennessee, but they also provide a rare first-hand account of the final days of John Armfield, one of the most notorious domestic slave traders in American history. They are of great value to both genealogists and historians alike, who will be grateful to Martin for having carefully compiled and annotated them here."

Joshua D. Rothman—Professor and Chair, History Dept., University of Alabama. Author of several books, including *Flush Times and Fever Dreams: A Story of Capitalism and Slavery in the Age of Jackson*, University of Georgia Press, 2012.

"Using the letters, Martin has written a charming tribute to two families and the heritage they perpetuated. Along the way, the book becomes a story rich in the history of a time and place and does not skimp on the rough spots. The magnificent, annotated collection of photographs fleshes out the story of additional generations. The Preface to 'Love's Young Dream' addresses the much-neglected problem of writing about families ensconced in a culture dominated by slavery and Jim Crow."

Judith Hillman Paterson—Instructor 20 years, Philip Merrill College of Journalism. Author of several books, including *Sweet Mystery: A Book of Remembering*, University of Alabama Press, 2001.

"Readers will see the Franklin family as the real, complicated people they were—vital and passionate, deeply caring and yet, clearly, people of their times. The letters are a treat, but the usefulness to historians and others comes from Martin's masterful command of the context. He does a great job of making sure that even the passing references in the letters are clear to readers. This is a must-have for anybody interested in Middle Tennessee history."

Betsy Phillips—Writer/contributor, *The Washington Post* and *Nashville Scene*. Author of *A City of Ghosts*, Createspace Independent Publishing, 2010.

"Martin lays an historical and genealogical foundation leading to a collection of romantic letters from his great-great-grandfather, Dr. Edward Noel Franklin, to his future bride, Nannie Hillman. Despite a great Civil War during their formative years, their families provided for them quality educations, enabling them to lead fulfilling lives. Here is recorded a genteel love story of the late nineteenth century revealing a way of life in Victorian Tennessee."

Kenneth Calvin Thomson, Jr.—Historian of Sumner County. Author (with Dee Gee Lester) of *Around Gallatin and Sumner County, Volumes 1 and 2*, "Images of America" series, Arcadia Publishing, 1996.

"Love's Young Dream"

*The Letters of Dr. Edward Noel Franklin
to Miss Nannie Hillman ~1871~*

"Love's Young Dream"

*The Letters of Dr. Edward Noel Franklin
to Miss Nannie Hillman ~1871~*

Edited with Introduction and Afterword by Terry L. Martin

Gallatin, Tennessee

~~~~~~~~

"Love's Young Dream": The Letters of Dr. Edward Noel Franklin
to Miss Nannie Hillman—1871

Edited with Introduction and Afterword by Terry L. Martin.

Copyright © 2018 Terry L. Martin

All rights reserved. Manufactured in the United States of America.
For permissions contact the editor:
tmartin@silvergobletpress.com

BISAC:
HIS036050 History / United States / Civil War Period (1850-1877)
HIS036120 History / United States / State & Local / South
HIS054000 History / Social History

ISBN: 978-1-7320138-0-3 (Hardcover) Special Edition—large, full-color
ISBN: 978-1-7320138-1-0 (Paperback) Grayscale

Library of Congress Control Number: 2018935736

Cover design by Susan Hofsass Sneed
Cover photo images: Dr. Edward Noel Franklin (1846-1909),
Nannie Hillman (1847-1923),
Edward and Nannie Wedding Portrait (1872)

Gallatin, Tennessee, USA
www.silvergobletpress.com

For All the Family

Contents

Preface 3

Introduction 5

The Letters of Edward to Nannie 17

Afterword 73

Photographs 81

Appendix 1, Articles on the Case of *Franklin v. Franklin* 115

Appendix 2, Articles on 1871 Beersheba Springs 131

Legacy: An Essay on Slavery by the Editor.........................141

Acknowledgements 145

Sources 147

For Further Reading 169

Index 171

Reference Charts:

Chart A—The Hillman Clan (Nannie's Family)—page 6
Chart B—The Franklin Clan (Edward's Family)—page 9
Chart C—Children and Grandchildren of Edward and Nannie—page 78

Preface

The purpose of this volume is three-fold. Firstly and most significantly, it is a snapshot in time, a picture of the early 1870s, a blossoming love affair, the interconnection of families. Century-and-a-half-old letters should be preserved, but, more importantly, read, in order to bring that past more vividly to life. Here we find the struggles of transportation on mountain roads, flipped carriages, annoyance with the postal service, and struggles with death of close family members. We also find humor, reference to parties, hunting, family and social gatherings, and thoughtful tenderness. We find a man in love.

Secondly, it is local history with regional and even national connections. There are many records, paintings, and photos that help define the story of the Franklin and Hillman families, prominent families of the Nashville greater area. Most particularly there is an emphasis on Sumner County, Grundy County, and Nashville, with stretches out to the Empire Iron Works in Trigg County, Kentucky and in the area now known as the Land Between the Lakes, where the Hillmans prospered. These were families that hands-on advanced the development of these places.

Did these clans take advantage of slavery in achieving what they did? Absolutely. Though the letters reflect a brief period in 1871, six years after the Civil War and slavery had ended, the stories of the families of Edward Noel Franklin and Nannie Hillman go back long before—the Franklins themselves to the settlement of central Tennessee in the 1770s. The first Franklins shot at and likely killed Indians in order to take possession of their claims. We therefore cannot deny the sacrifice of Native Americans, either.

And I say "absolutely" with emphasis in the case of the Franklins and the Hillmans. More detail is presented in the Introduction and in the photo captions as to the extent slavery advanced the wealth of these families.

Which brings me to the third purpose of presenting these letters and explains their national significance. Edward's letters contain a first-hand account of the final days of the infamous slave trader, John Armfield. Edward gives in these letters an account of his

Uncle Armfield's final days and death, as he was present when he died. Modern historical research is placing emphasis on uncovering the details of the slave-trading empire of the Alexandria, Virginia-based Franklin and Armfield firm, and any primary source materials of this nature are of benefit to those researchers.

As important as the Armfield material is, Nannie's family, the Hillmans, fit prominently into the national fabric, too. Hillman iron played a significant role in the South as the Civil War was heating up, even more so afterward, and much too has been written on the family's role in the industrial development of Birmingham and Pittsburgh. The Pittsburgh Hillmans are important to this day and have philanthropic foundations scattered about the country. Yet less emphasis has been placed on the historical background of the family, and the Introduction and photograph captions purport to assist in that.

Though lengthier biographies could be written, the focus here is on Edward's letters, and it is my hope that most readers will be encouraged by the love Edward demonstrates to Nannie. It is indeed a snapshot in time. This tells us something of Beersheba Springs, of Nashville, and of Sumner County in 1871. The Introduction and the Afterword give sufficient detail for a work of this limited scope. Family charts are provided in order to assist the reader with names and relationships, and the photograph section is fantastic for giving a visual and for detailing the story. Annotations are meant to be elaborative for the reader. A comprehensive list acknowledging over 190 different sources is arranged alphabetically by person or subject in order to easily find referenced materials and spur further research. Transcribed in two appendices are historical periodical articles on the fanciful resort at Beersheba Springs and on the sensational Gallatin and state Supreme Court case of *Franklin v. Franklin* between Edward and his father. I end with an essay entitled, "Legacy," a contribution to the modern-day, slavery-reconciliation conversation.

Introduction

They were prominent families. The Franklins, the Hillmans, the Marables, the Gentrys and the Armfields were some of Middle Tennessee's best known. Wealth and status revolved around them. Though they lost much wealth during the Civil War, much of it was reclaimed after. Descendants of some of these families are still found in Middle Tennessee, particularly in Davidson and Sumner Counties, and then there are the Hillmans of Pittsburgh, Pennsylvania. African Americans, descendants of those enslaved by the families prior to the war, often bear their surnames. Franklins and Hillmans, certainly. Gentrys, too, and with the Marable family in particular, it is believed more African-Americans bear the surname today than whites descended from the original plantation-owning families.

The families came from the east, of course, Maryland and Virginia for the most part, though the Hillmans hailed from New Jersey. The Marables were some of the early English settlers in 1600's Jamestown, Virginia. A century and a half later, the Rev. Henry Hartwell Marable came to Tennessee and built a large log cabin in Smyrna, in which years later would be born the Confederate soldier and scout, Sam Davis. This cabin was in recent times moved to the rear of the Historic Sam Davis Home and Plantation and is eventually to be restored and used as interpretive space. Henry's son, John Hartwell Marable, was a doctor and a U.S. Congressman who represented Clarksville for two terms during the John Quincy Adams years. He married Ann Jones Watson, and it was their daughter, Ann Jones Marable, who married into the wealthy Hillman family.

An elder Daniel Hillman lived in a number of locales after leaving New Jersey. He died in Alabama after opening an iron works west of present-day Birmingham at what is now known as Tannehill Ironworks Historical State Park. His history is interpreted there at the Iron and Steel Museum of Alabama. His sons, Daniel, Jr., among them, came to Tennessee, opening iron works in sundry locations west of Nashville, and later in Trigg and Lyon Counties, Kentucky, in the area that is now Land Between the Lakes National Recreation Area. Ruins from some of these old works still exist. At one point,

Reference Chart A.
The Hillman Clan—Nannie's Family

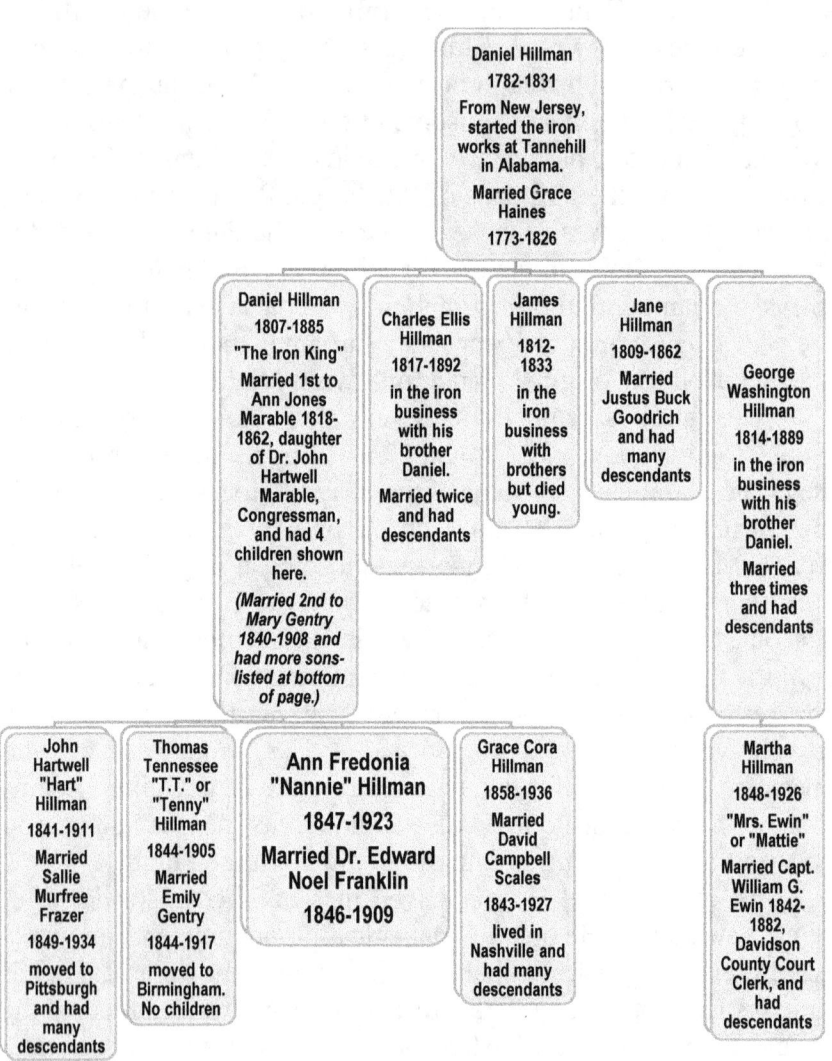

Nannie's half-siblings by way of her father Daniel's second wife, Mary Gentry, are as follows: Daniel C. Hillman (1867-1889), Meredith Poindexter Gentry Hillman (1868-1944), James Hoggatt Hillman (1870-1918), and Bellfield Carter Hillman (1875-1876). A eulogy of Mary mentions a daughter who did not survive. Daniel is known to have fathered two other children: Mary Ann Hillman Barbour (1834-1873), who was raised in the home, and John W. Hillman (1848-1911), whose African-American mother is presumed to have been enslaved.

records show Daniel had more enslaved workers than any other enterprise, industrial or agricultural, in the state of Kentucky, many leased from other owners. He lost a fortune in the war, and though he recreated much of it in the late 1860s, there were slow periods in the 1870s in which he feared bankruptcy. In 1840 he married Ann Jones Marable. Together, they produced two sons, John Hartwell and Thomas Tennessee, and two daughters, Grace Cora and her older sister Ann Fredonia, known by everyone as "Nannie."

Their mother Ann died of consumption during the war in 1862, but three years later widower Daniel and his son T.T.[1] met up with a pair of prominent Nashville sisters, Mary and Emily. These were the daughters of Meredith Poindexter Gentry, a long-serving U.S. Congressman and unsuccessful 1855 candidate for governor against Andrew Johnson. The tale goes that Daniel took T.T. to meet Mary with the intention of setting those two up for a marital union, but on the return journey home, Daniel admitted being so impressed by her that he told his son he was not allowed to marry her, for he himself had decided upon marrying her instead! T.T. resorted to marrying the younger sister, Emily. Subsequently, Daniel and Mary produced additional children, all boys. Certainly there were relationships with these much younger half-brothers, nevertheless the first four from their Marable mother—T.T., 'Hart', Nannie, and Grace—remained particularly close for the rest of their lives. Eventually, T.T. and Emily moved to Birmingham, Alabama, where T.T. was hugely influential in establishing the steel industry by way of his investments in the Alice Furnaces among other enterprises. Concurrently, older brother Hart did somewhat the same in Pittsburgh, Pennsylvania. Though T.T. and Emily had no children to carry on his legacy, Hart did. His descendants broadened their investments, becoming billionaires, Calgon Carbon and The Hillman Company being the descendent businesses, and these Hillmans are scattered about the country, some still in Pittsburgh. In any event, Nannie and Grace in time benefited enormously by way of their brothers' generosity, investment advice, and financial expertise.

---

[1] Thomas Tennessee Hillman, in addition to being called T. T., was also called "Tenny" by family members.

Nannie's suitor and author of these letters, Dr. Edward Noel Franklin, was the great-grandson of James Franklin, a corporal from the Revolution, who settled his land grant in Sumner County, Tennessee. Fighting off Indian attacks, James was designated by James Robertson, founder of Nashville, as one of the Immortal Seventy, a group of white settlers who survived these violent years of Middle Tennessee's earliest political history. Eventually James and his sons bought thousands of acres between Gallatin and old Saundersville (now a part of Hendersonville), and several old Franklin homes can still be seen there today. James' grave near his home Pilot Knob on Station Camp Creek was restored in 2016 by the General Jethro Sumner Chapter of the Daughters of the American Revolution.[2]

James had ten children by his wife Mary Lauderdale,[3] herself from a very prominent Virginia family, but the most famous, or infamous, of these was Isaac.

Isaac Franklin connected in a partnership with John Armfield, a former stagecoach operator from North Carolina. Family ties were cemented when Armfield followed Isaac home to Sumner County and married his niece, Martha Franklin. Much has been written about these characters by historians studying the American Slave Trade, and from the research we find that Franklin and Armfield were two of the most notorious and biggest slave traders of their time, purchasing thousands of slaves in Virginia and Maryland. From headquarters in Alexandria, Virginia, slave coffles either marched southwest (through Gallatin and Nashville) or boarded a fleet of boats, destined for Natchez and New Orleans where slavery was expanding rapidly. There, they were resold at enormous profit. But by the 1840s, Franklin and Armfield were out of the business, and within a few short years Isaac was dead with small children who did not survive to adulthood.[4] Some historians have concluded that his wife Adelicia was the wealthiest widow in the nation at her first husband's death. Though she eventually sold their Fairvue plantation in Gallatin, for a time she kept the five cotton

---

[2] Pilot Knob, greatly modified, is now Golden Era Plantation on Saundersville Road in Hendersonville. The restored grave is nearby in Saundersville Station subdivision.

[3] James also fathered a Franklin son by another woman.

[4] There is also evidence Isaac fathered a child by a female slave, Lucindy, both mother and son whom he sent out of the way to Louisville before Adelicia came to live with him at Fairvue. (See information on the book, *The Half Has Never Been Told,* by Edward Baptist in "Sources" list.)

Reference Chart B.
The Franklin Clan—Edward's Family

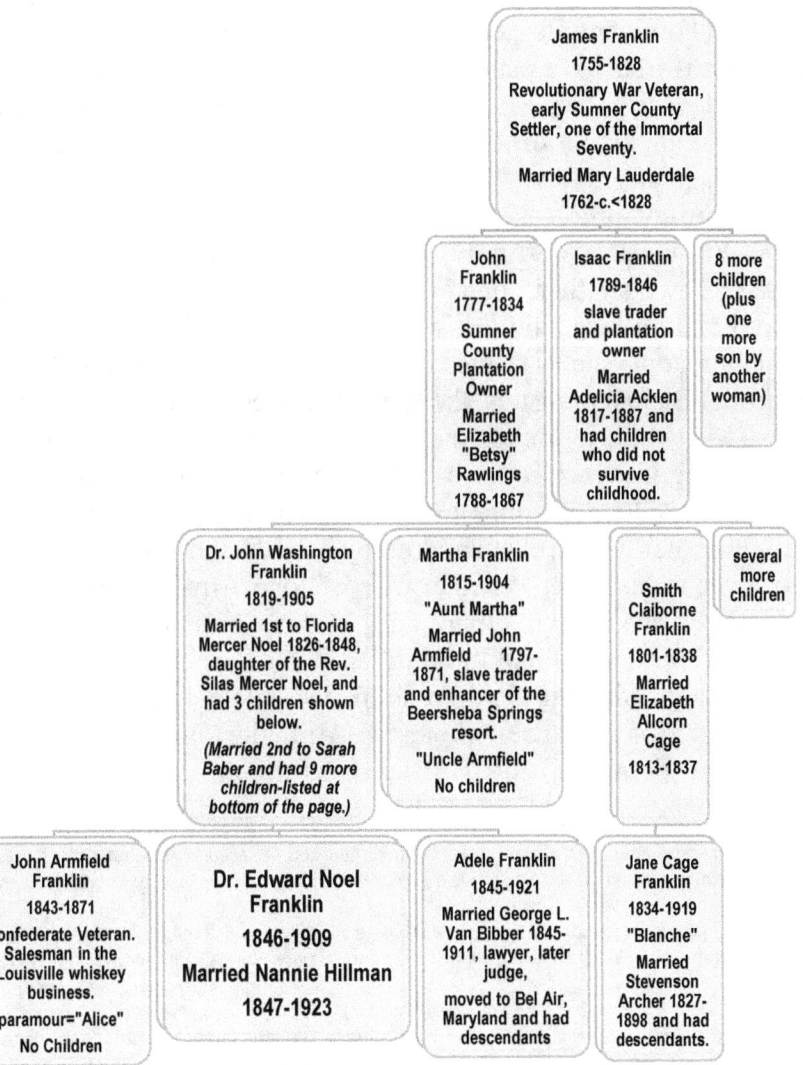

Edward's half-siblings by way of his father's second wife, Sarah Baber, are as follows: Lucien Baber Franklin, Sr. (1850-1924), Ernest Franklin (1855-1931), Thomas Baber Franklin (1857-1934), Blanche Franklin Burwell (1861-1945), Lina Franklin (1863-1871), James W. Franklin (1864-1934), Robert Lee Franklin (1866-1920), Benjamin Hallowell Franklin (1868-1949), and Mabel Franklin (1872-1947).

plantations in Louisiana, married secondly to Joseph Acklen, and built Belmont in Nashville. She is without a doubt a Scarlett O'Hara-like figure, and much has been written about her.

But there were other Franklins. Another son of patriarch James, and brother to Isaac, was John Franklin, also a Sumner County plantation owner.[5] He married Elizabeth Rawlings, and one of their sons, John Washington Franklin, grew up to become a doctor. Edward Noel Franklin, author of these letters, was John Washington's son. It was through his father's influence that Edward himself chose the medical profession.

Yet most interestingly, Edward, born October 20, 1846, was not raised by his father. John Washington's first wife, and mother of Edward and his two siblings, was Florida Mercer Noel of Frankfort and Lexington. She was the daughter of one of Kentucky's most influential Baptist ministers, the Rev. Silas Mercer Noel.[6] Edward was born at Maywood, a brick home in downtown Gallatin,[7] but two years later, having moved briefly to New Orleans, his mother died in that city of typhus. John Washington, returning promptly to the mid-south, then chose not to keep his children by Florida and instead delivered them over to his sister, Martha, wife of John Armfield. Having no children of their own, John and Martha became the surrogate parents of the three Franklin children, which included a namesake elder brother, John Armfield Franklin, and Adele, their sister.[8] There was another, older cousin whom the Armfields also helped raise—Jane Cage Franklin, called "Blanche."[9] Soon, John Washington

---

[5] The John Franklin home, "Woodlawn," was demolished and replaced in the first half of the 20th century. Sometimes called Wilson Farm or the Comer House, it is now the Sumner County Convention and Visitor's Bureau on Nashville Pike.

[6] Silas M. Noel was a key founder of Georgetown College and a powerful defender of traditional Baptist faith against the Stone-Campbell Restoration Movement. His wife, Florida's mother, was Maria Waring Noel.

[7] Maywood today is often called 'The Trousdale-Baskerville House'. It is located at the corner of South Locust and West Smith Streets in Gallatin near to the Sumner County museum. It is not to be confused with Trousdale Place, immediately in front of the museum on West Main Street.

[8] Though true that Martha Armfield had no children, recent DNA evidence suggests John Armfield produced descendants by way of an enslaved African-American. See references under "Armfield Family" in "Sources."

[9] Jane Cage (Blanche) Franklin (1834-1919) was the daughter of Smith Claiborne Franklin (a brother to Martha Armfield and to John Washington Franklin) and of his wife, Elizabeth Cage Franklin. Both parents died when Blanche was a small child. Though according to Isabel Howell's biography of Armfield, Blanche was under the guardianship of John Sanderson (another relative) this was probably just a

Franklin married again, this time to Sarah Baber of another plantation family near Gallatin.[10] It makes some sense John Washington, initially desperate after the death of Florida, would have turned to his sister as a mother-figure for his children, who were still small. Yet unlike Blanche's case, whose parents had both died young, it is a mystery why, after procuring his new wife, John Washington's children were not brought back into his home. It was certainly not due to lack of adequate finances. For, upon his remarriage, he built for Sarah a Gothic-inspired brick mansion, Oakley, in sight of the Baber plantation. This fine home still stands today, not far from Isaac's Fairvue, very close to Volunteer State Community College. With Sarah, John Washington produced nine more children, and during the war he served as a physician in the Confederate Army.

For a time, the Armfields with the Franklin children lived at "Hard Times," another antebellum home not far from Franklin lands.[11] John Armfield made improvements on the farm and also helped to execute Isaac Franklin's will. However, within a few years, Armfield took his substantial wealth from the slave trade and invested in the enhancement of the resort and a home at Beersheba Springs, Tennessee, atop the Cumberland Plateau. It quickly became famous, as wealthy Southerners flocked there in the summers from near and far. Yet war came within two years of the refurbishment. Its buildings were robbed and vandalized many times, and though afterwards Armfield and the family continued living there and reopened the hotel, not in his remaining years did it achieve quite its pre-war grandiosity. The Armfield home where most of Edward's letters were written is still there, as is the hotel complex. The old hotel buildings belong today to the Tennessee Conference of the United Methodist Church, and have been the site of innumerable mountain-top retreats by youth representing that faith tradition.

---

financial arrangement over her inheritance from her deceased parents. It is plain that the Armfields acted as parents to her, as Armfield himself says so in his will. Blanche, along with Martha and the other three Franklin children, were in the will, each to receive a 20% share of his estate. In 1854 or 1855, Blanche married Stevenson Archer, a lawyer from Maryland.

[10] The Baber plantation was called Bellemont, although it should not be confused with Adelicia's Belmont in Nashville. The Baber home is now known as Foxland Hall, today containing a fine-dining restaurant overlooking Old Hickory Lake.

[11] "Hard Times" is now known as Spring Haven Mansion in Hendersonville, a popular wedding and reception venue.

The Franklin children grew up then in Sumner and Grundy counties, wintering sometimes in Louisiana, or were away at boarding school, and despite the fact John Washington maintained continual contact with these his children from his first wife, for all practical purposes the Armfields, John and Martha, were the primary caregivers. They provided the needed mother and father role models. It is true, however, that the three, particularly Adele, would sometimes visit their father and stepmother at Oakley.

The Armfield family appear to have been close, and in time the Franklin children reached adulthood. Armfield's namesake, the eldest of the three, was a soldier in the Confederate Army. An interesting and passionate character, John Armfield Franklin spent four years in the army in the 7th Tennessee Infantry, seeing much action, transferring in the last months of the war to the 13th Virginia Cavalry. He was present to the end, surrendering his arms finally at Appomattox. His diary fragments exist from that time. After the war, he was employed as a drummer[12] in the whiskey business in Louisville, and while there he became enamored of a woman by the name of "Alice." Though Edward in these letters mentions this woman as his brother's wife, and apparently John Armfield Franklin passed her off as such, as eventually became publicly known, theirs was not a relationship within the 'holy bounds of matrimony.' She was but his paramour who traveled about with him. Taken altogether, the tidbits of biographical information on this brother would create the basis for a rather interesting novel.

The two brothers were deeply devoted to their sister, Adele. She received part of her education at Nashville Female Academy and was at times head of her class. Eventually she was sent to Patapsco Institute, a girls' finishing school in Ellicott City, Maryland. While there, she visited her cousin Blanche, who had married Stevenson Archer some years before the war. They introduced Adele to Archer's nephew, George Lindenberger Van Bibber, who would graduate from Princeton and go on to become a lawyer in partnership with Archer. Shortly before Edward's first long letter was written in August of 1871, Adele married Van Bibber in Beersheba Springs, and moved with him to his home in Bel Air, Maryland. Yet before she married

---

[12] A salesman, as in the phrase 'drummed up business'.

and moved away, the letters imply she had developed a close friendship with Nannie Hillman.

This first daughter of Daniel and Ann Jones Marable Hillman, born in Montgomery County, Tennessee on October 19, 1847, was diminutive in frame with a sweet Southern Belle face and light, strawberry blond hair. As a 12-year-old girl she traveled to New Orleans and was, perhaps as an enjoyable aside on the part of her father or mother, taken to a Professor O. S. Fowler for an interview. He, in addition to quizzing her, very possibly analyzed her facial features and measured the dimensions of her skull. He then wrote up Nannie's "Phrenological Character":

This girl is exceedingly sensitive—one of the most fine-grained—delicate—susceptible girls I examine—Is most intense in her desires—wants what she wants at all like a house on fire—Does what she does at all with railroad speed—Is positive in all her likes and dislikes—Is always in a hurry—Is as light on foot as a deer—is too impetuous—too variable—like April weather—and needs unity—and harmony—but when good—is one of the best of girls—one perfect bundle of Love—one of the kindest—most obliging—most sympathetic—tender feeling—but her anger is equally positive and very flashy—still is quick over—like gunpowder—especially is terribly cut—or provoked if you blame her—ought not to be found fault with—Is gratified beyond measure if you commend her—does her very best—so that she deserves commendation and her faults are only the out-gushings of her strong feeling—not intentional—and every time you blame her you lose ground—so just talk through her intellect to her moral sentiments and better feelings—She takes most of her characteristics from her mother and mother's father—and on that side is derived from a very long-lived strong-constitutioned family—she is exceedingly fond of children—has a perfect passion for doll babies—will be one of the most motherly of mothers—and affectionate of wives—provided her affections are drawn upon...[13]

---

[13] Phrenology was a pseudoscientific forerunner of psychology, popular in the 1800s. In large part the idea was to analyze human character based on facial features, the shape and dimensions of the skull, bumps on the head, and to make comparisons with successful people, criminals, etc. Professor Fowler was an eminent proponent of the theory during his day, writing several books and contributing to journals. A sizeable collection of phrenology works is displayed at the historic Thomas Hughes Free Public Library in Rugby, Tennessee, including several by Fowler. Based in New York, Fowler apparently

This charming piece continues for several more pages. Nannie is mentioned several times (by the name "Annie") in *The Diary of Nannie Haskins Williams: A Southern Woman's Story of Rebellion and Reconstruction, 1863-1890* (ed. Uffelman, et al., UT Press, 2014). After visiting this friend in Union Army-occupied Clarksville one day in 1863, our Nannie is described by this other Nannie in oddly contradictory terms: "…I practiced with Annie Hillman this evening. She is Mattie's cousin who is going to school with her. I think she is one of the nicest girls I ever saw. She is not at all pretty—in any estimation looks do not constitute beauty. Such beautiful rosy cheeks she has and elegant eyes; neither her mouth nor her nose are pretty. Some would admire her hair, but I would not. It is real flaxen. So far as I have seen her I think I will admire her more than I do Mattie though I love the latter dearly…"[14]

Our Nannie was well educated. She and her cousin, Mattie (Martha Jane) Hillman,[15] were sent by their wealthy fathers away from the on-going war to Chegaray Institute, a French boarding school in Philadelphia. This is confirmed a few months later in the same diary: "…They will start back to Philadelphia tomorrow. They are going on to school to a French woman 'Madam Masse.' They wanted me to go with them, but no indeed I would not go to Yankeedom to school…" Unlike the diary author's firmly pro-Confederate family, the Hillman clan had fewer compunctions about making northern connections.[16] Bound volumes of music in the editor's collection embossed with Nannie's name and school indicate music was an important pursuit for her. Nannie certainly owned and read books in French, and knew needlework and quilting. She also appears to have had a good head for

---

would travel sometimes to New Orleans. The quoted document is the original, from the editor's collection.

[14] This diary by Nannie Haskins Williams was repeatedly referenced in Ken Burn's PBS series on the Civil War. See "Ewin Family" or "Franklin, Nannie" in 'Sources.' See also 'For Further Reading.'

[15] Mattie (Martha Jane Hillman) was the daughter of George Washington Hillman, Daniel's brother, and of Susan, George's second wife. She was thus Nannie's first cousin, and the two appear to have been close. Mattie later married Capt. William G. Ewin. Since the Ewins are mentioned frequently in Edward's letters, see the footnote on the Ewins in Letter 18.

[16] Since the fall of Forts Donelson and Henry to the Union Army in 1862, Hillman-manufactured iron from the nearby works had been rerouted from Southern to Northern interests. However, the output eventually slowed to a stop, as many of the slaves employed at the works had run away or sought protection by Union officials and been freed. The Hillmans lost a fortune during the war, but even during the worst of it they were still relatively wealthy.

math and money management, confirmed by the expense journals she later kept. In 1867, probably while still in Philadelphia, Nannie sat for Samuel Bell Waugh, who had already painted Lincoln and would soon paint Grant. Despite what her Clarksville friend may have said in her diary four years earlier, by this time Nannie's appearance in this portrait by the famed artist is captivating. At nineteen, going on twenty, she had grown into a very lovely woman indeed.[17]

It appears likely it was by way of Nannie's aforementioned friendship with his sister Adele that Edward came to know Nannie. They certainly could have met in Nashville in the past, and Nannie visited Beersheba Springs that summer of 1871 at the time of Adele's wedding. Clearly, that spring and summer was when the relationship between Edward and Nannie blossomed. As indicated in the very first short note in May, he sent her rose buds—he later affectionately called her his "rose bud"—in thanks for the picture of herself that she had sent him, and this exchange of favoritism marks the official beginning of their love affair.

By this time, Edward had been an M.D. two years. He had attended boarding school, paid for by his father, at Forest Home Academy, Jefferson County, Kentucky. He then studied medicine under his father, later attending the University of Pennsylvania, where he received his M.D. in 1869. After graduating, Edward went to Texas for a time, serving in a hospital in Galveston. Yet soon he returned home to Tennessee to nurse "Uncle Armfield" at Beersheba Springs, whose health had begun to decline. Edward of course served as the physician at the resort, though, as shown in the letters, he did travel occasionally 'off the mountain' to others who requested his services. Not counting the first, brief thank-you note from mid-May, the first real letter, dated August 13, 1871, was written ten days following the marriage of his sister Adele to George Van Bibber. *The Examiner* newspaper of Gallatin from Saturday, August 19, 1871, reported the wedding having taken place at the Armfield home in Beersheba Springs: "…It was a most magnificent affair, rivalling the good old times that distinguished our country before the war…"

---

[17] This painting of Nannie by Waugh is reproduced in the photograph section.

The same newspaper also lists the important guests at the resort that summer.[18] In the paragraph featuring the prominent lady visitors, "the charming and beautiful Miss Nannie Hillman, of Nashville," is listed second only to "the elegant and imperial Mrs. Gen. John H. Morgan" whose husband of Morgan's Raiders fame had of course been killed in the war. None of the rest of the ladies in the list were given any such grand descriptors. No doubt Edward believed himself the luckiest man in Middle Tennessee to find himself engaged to such an eligible damsel as Nannie Hillman. Her father was called the "Iron King," and Edward had struck gold with the princess.

---

[18] This article from *The Examiner,* which gives much information about 1871 Beersheba Springs, is transcribed in Appendix 2.

The Letters of Dr. Edward Noel Franklin to Miss Nannie Hillman –1871

Editing Parameters

The preserved quality of the original letters varies considerably. Whereas some are easily readable with dark ink on white stationery, a number are on blue stationery and with lighter ink. Some were water-damaged, splotched and faded. Nevertheless, with care, they can all still be read and deciphered. There is an example of Edward's cursive shown in one of the photographs, and after a little, I found it reasonably easy to transcribe.

In this printed version, I have chosen to combine Edward's use of double word forms into their typical singular word forms such as "every body" into "everybody," "to day" into "today," "when ever" into "whenever," etc.

All the underlining and punctuation are Edward's with some exceptions. I have added periods after Mrs., Mr., Dr., Messrs., and others. Misspelled words are left in place, marked "(sic)". Where Edward places the contraction accent symbol is certainly not considered correct today, as he always placed it before the "nt" rather than between the "n" and "t," such as in "have not" which he rendered "have'nt." I have corrected to "haven't." In contrast, he did not place an accent in the contractions "can't" and "don't," but I have done so. Sometimes he would abbreviate a name or place name with its first letter, knowing Nannie knew whom or where he meant, but I have completed the rest of the name in parentheses following, for instance, "Aunt M(artha)".

There are 27 letters. The first is really a thank-you note from May. The next is dated August 13, ten days following Edward's sister Adele's marriage to George Van Bibber in Beersheba Springs. This letter he actually describes as his 'first letter' to Nannie.

--Terry Martin, January 17, 2018

Love's Young Dream

By Thomas Moore (1779-1852)

Oh! the days are gone, when Beauty bright
    My heart's chain wove;
When my dream of life, from morn till night,
    Was love, still love.
    New hope may bloom,
    And days may come,
  Of milder calmer beam,
But there's nothing half so sweet in life
    As love's young dream:
No, there's nothing half so sweet in life
    As love's young dream.

Though the bard to purer fame may soar,
    When wild youth's past;
Though he win the wise, who frown'd before,
    To smile at last;
    He'll never meet
    A joy so sweet,
  In all his noon of fame,
As when first he sung to woman's ear
    His soul-felt flame,
And, at every close, she blush'd to hear
    The one loved name.

No, -- that hallow'd form is ne'er forgot
    Which first love traced;
Still it lingering haunts the greenest spot
    On memory's waste.
    'Twas odour fled
    As soon as shed;
  'Twas morning's winged dream;
'Twas a light, that ne'er can shine again
    On life's dull stream:
Oh! 'twas light that n'er can shine again
    On life's dull stream.

Letter 1

    Please accept my compliments Miss Nannie accompanied with the promised moss-rose buds.
    Your picture I received, and for it I return my lone heart's warmest thanks. I assure you it recalled very many pleasant reminiscences of the much cherished past. You could not possibly have bestowed it upon anyone by whom it would have been more highly appreciated.
    With much respect I am

                  Very truly
                      Your friend
                          Ed N. Franklin.

"Beersheba Springs."
May 16th / '71.

Letter 2

Beersheba.
Sunday, Aug 13th/'71.

Miss Nannie.

Your letter received a warm welcome at my hands last evening, and I can say with truth that never in my life have I received a letter that gave me more pleasure. I knew you would write, felt convinced that you would, and yet could not help feeling just a little anxious about it. Am so much obliged that you did not disappoint me. I thought you would tell Mrs. Ewin[19] all, and am glad you did so. Think when I tell her about the "serious question," she will see it in quite a different light. <u>Of course</u> you could tell it, as if there was nothing to laugh at.

The masquerade ball was a decided success; the costumes were, most of them, very pretty and becoming,[20] the supper <u>beautiful</u>, and "all went merry as a marriage bell."[21] Although I enjoyed it very much, my thoughts would wander back to other evenings when I was far happier, – made so by the "absent friend,"[22] – and I thought of a face, brighter far, than any I could see on that occasion. So far from being "oblivious to that absent Sister[23] and friend," I thought of them so much that I had to be reminded several times, by a very fair representation of aurora,[24] that I was not listening to what she was saying to me. Would give you a full description of the affair, and tell you who and what each one represented, but know you will see it all in either the Banner or Union American, as they both had reporters present who were busy

---

[19] Mrs. Ewin is Mattie, Nannie's cousin. Since Capt. and Mrs. Ewin are mentioned frequently beginning with Letter 18, see the detailed footnote there.
[20] The ball was held at the Beersheba Springs hotel. Edward dressed as 'Don Cesar de Bazan'.
[21] From the poem "The Eve of Waterloo," by Lord Byron (1788-1824).
[22] Nannie is of course the 'absent friend'. Common literary reference possibly originating with the poem, "An Absent Friend" by Sappho (c.630-c.570 BC).
[23] This references his sister Adele who recently married and moved away.
[24] Miss Jennie Winston dressed as "Aurora" at the ball.

taking notes all evening; and I had rather devote my letter to something you cannot get from a news-paper.[25]

I cannot begin to tell you how much we miss both Sister and yourself. Every time I come in, I feel like walking on tip-toe and talking in a whisper; really it seems like there has been a death in the house.

That morning after the train[26] containing all I loved upon earth, had "vanished like a dream,"[27] leaving me "alone to weep the silent tear,"[28] I wended my way back to the hotêl de ville, with a "still, small voice"[29] whispering in my ear, another tie broken. I felt sad, very sad, and yet was not altogether unhappy. Feelings of sorrow and happiness seemed blended, for when I thought of my Sister, lost to me forever, "my poor heart was sad with its dreaming"[30]; but when I thought of you, my newly found treasure, my poor heart was sad no longer, but was made glad. I believe I have loved my Sister as devoutly as a Sister was ever loved, but I felt that at the same time I had lost her, I had found one who I could love even more fondly.

After sitting quietly down, and <u>smoking a cigar</u>, I felt quite myself again and immediately repaired to the "lawyers row"[31] and interviewed Mr. Clark,[32] with a view to bringing him to the "giddy mountain top," but soon discovered he could not leave McMinnville on any account. I did not demolish him as I had threatened to do in case he refused, but let him live to love a certain young lady who, he informed me, has grown very fond of him of late. But enough of Mr. Clark. I concluded, as I could do no better, to "go it alone," and try to put up with my own company. As soon as this <u>noble</u> resolution

---

[25] The masquerade ball was featured in the *Republican Banner*, August, 13, 1871 and the *Nashville Union and American*, August 15, 1871, both highly-entertaining articles reproduced in Appendix 2.
[26] The McMinnville train station serviced most visitors to and from Beersheba Springs.
[27] From a poem and popular song of the time, "She Came and Vanished Like a Dream," by J. B. Boucher.
[28] Words likely originate from "The Silent Hour of Midnight," by George Walker (1772-1847).
[29] Biblical phrase.
[30] Popular song from 1867 entitled, "My Poor Heart is Sad With Its Dreaming," by T. Brigham Bishop.
[31] Likely a part of the hotel where the men gather to sleep or smoke, such as bunk rooms, a porch or smoking room.
[32] This is Richard Clark, the same mentioned in Letters 5 and 6, proprietor of the Tennessee Stave Factory in Battle Creek (and owner of Beersheba Springs Hotel). See footnote in Letter 6.

had been formed, I proceeded to put the daring fete into execution; and started, bearing a very forlorn countenance. The Sun shone, the birds sang, and all nature seemed smiling at my long face, so I just thought I would put it off at once, and immediately commenced to sing all the comic songs I could think of, and in the course of a very brief space of time was feeling "just as happy as a big sun-flower."[33]

     I hope you will pardon me for intruding one verse of a very ridiculous parody, I perpetrated on bidding you good-bye at the depot. It goes thusly---

We parted by the mountain side,
The Sun looked down on you and me,
   Sister put on a look of pride,
And Williams murmured unto thee;
   George smiled upon the blushing bride,
And gentle Steve did sigh,
   One word broke Nannie's sweet repose,
That sad word was – Good-bye.[34]

     And now Miss Nannie as this is my first letter I must try not to weary you if I have not done so already, but bring this unfortunate production to a termination; not without a heart full of affection, however, for each member of your family, and a double amount for yourself.

     Thanks for the assurance that the letter to your father shall be delivered promptly. Aunt M(artha)[35] received your letter last night, and I presume, will write soon.

     Please write to me very soon.

     May the indulgent gods hover around your couch this night and fill your slumbers with golden visions of your absent friend,

                   Ed N. Franklin.

---

[33] Line from popular song entitled, "The Big Sunflower," by Billy Newcomb (1847-1888).
[34] The lines are original by Edward. "Sister" and "blushing bride" are Adele, "George" is her new husband, "Nannie" is obvious, "Williams" and "Steve" may be real persons, but may be generic male names, representing other men trying to gain Nannie's attention.
[35] Martha Franklin Armfield, Edward's aunt, wife to John Armfield.

Letter 3

Beersheba.
Aug 15th/'71

Miss Nannie.

I received your letter on Saturday night, – as I <u>knew</u> I would – and wrote to you on Sunday, enclosing a letter of <u>importance</u> to your Father.

Have just received the enclosed letter from Mrs. Nash, and make it an excuse for writing you a short note; it makes the second I have enclosed to you since you left: hope you will get both. Took it for granted you had left Nashville, and directed my letter to the Iron Works,[36] as I will do this one also; though I believe Aunt Martha wrote you one on yesterday and directed to Nashville.

Have just had a sweet letter from Sister, written at home. She had improved very much, and was feeling quite herself again. They left for Baltimore[37] on Friday evening. She said in her letter to me, that she had just finished one to yourself; hope you have received it.

My horse – "Don" – died last night, the trip to McMinnville was too much for him. I believe I told you going down that he was not well.

Think I am having all my bad luck at one time – lost my Sister, sweetheart and horse, all in less than one week. But as long as I have a hope of seeing my sweetheart again, I can very well stand the balance.

Believing you will write to me <u>very</u> soon, I am

Your <u>true</u> friend
Ed N. Franklin.

---

[36] The Empire Iron Works, Trigg County, Kentucky, location of Daniel Hillman's business operations and where he has a home. He also has a home in Nashville.
[37] His sister is moving to Bel Air, Maryland with her new husband, George Van Bibber.

Letter 4

Beersheba.
Aug 20th/'71

Miss Nannie.

    Although I have written to you twice in less than one week, for fear you should <u>forget</u> me, I beg leave to write you just a <u>short little letter</u> tonight. This has grown to be the most lonesome place in the world, and I must admit I am not a little selfish in writing to you, as it is done by way of entertaining myself; but your pity, I know, will move you to forgive me. As I do not know when you left Nashville, in fact do not know whether you have left at all or not, of course have no idea when I will hear from your father, but am content to await my time. Feel convinced all will be well.

    If such a thing is possible, I believe I love you more and more every day. You have grown to be a part of my very existence, and if deprived of your love I don't know what would become of me. You are "my heart's sweet home, my spirit's shrine."[38]

    Miss Jennie Winston[39] *says she <u>knows</u> possitively (sic) that I am to be married next fall to Miss Nannie, and that my attention to you was only a blind. <u>I can't fool her</u>? I took a drive with her last evening, and when I said something very <u>soft</u> to her she was horrified and insisted that she would tell Miss Nannie on me if I did not desist.*

    Messrs. Ewing[40] *and Lea*[41] *have left us now, and we are all alone in our glory. The house is like a "banquet hall deserted"*[42] *sure enough now. Aunt Martha was out last evening and I took tea all*

---

[38] From the poem, "Can You Forget Me?" by Letitia Elizabeth Landon (1802-1838).
[39] Miss Jennie went as "Aurora" to the Ball. She has been visiting Beersheba Springs for the summer with her father, Dr. J. D. Winston from Nashville. He is listed in newspaper ads as one of the doctors, along with Edward, who will be present that summer to administer to the vacationers. Jennie appears to enjoy teasing Edward about his romance with Nannie.
[40] Robert Ewing, a lawyer from Nashville, was at the Masquerade Ball dressed as 'Prince Leander'.
[41] Judge John M. Lea visited Beersheba that summer. He is known for having purchased the Claiborne mansion in Nashville in 1861 and donating it to the state to house the Tennessee School for the Blind.
[42] From "Oft in the Stilly Night," by Thomas Moore (1779-1852).

alone. Could not help contrasting the appearance of the table then and a week or two ago.[43] *Excuse a short letter and write soon to*

Your friend
Ed N. Franklin

---

[43] He is referencing his sister's wedding and banquet at the Armfield home on August 3.

Letter 5

Beersheba.
Aug 25th/'71.

Miss Nannie.

 Your letter, and one from your Father, was received tonight. His letter is everything I could ask. The only thing that mars the pleasure of this occasion is a knowledge of the <u>painful</u> fact that I haven't time to answer either letter, having just received a hasty summons to attend Mr. Clark who is dangerously ill over at Jasper. It is a drive of over forty miles, across the mountains; and I will be away several days, but as everything else is so lovely I don't mind it, and besides I have an excellent horse and buggy. My Father has made me a present of a very fine horse since the death of "Don Pedro."[44]

 Uncle Armfield[45] is not at all well and I cannot leave him for any length of time until Pa can come up and stay with him until my return; so you see I cannot tell when I can visit you, before I hear from him. Will write you all about it when I return from Jasper.

 Please return many thanks to your father for his kind invitation and say I will be most happy to accept it at my earliest convenience.

 But I must be off. <u>Excuse haste</u>, and accept all the love of

    Yours
    Ed N. Franklin.

---

[44] Edward's father, Dr. John Washington Franklin, a respected physician in Gallatin, also bred horses at his estate, Oakley, a common business practice among the Franklin kin.

[45] John Armfield, former slave trader, enhancer of Beersheba Springs resort, Edward's surrogate father and husband to Aunt Martha.

Letter 6

OFFICE OF

CLARK & BASS,
PROPRIETORS OF THE
TENNESSEE STAVE FACTORY

Battle Creek[46], Tenn., <u>Sunday Aug 27th</u>, 187 <u>1</u> .

Miss Nannie.

I wrote you a note from Beersheba the evening I received your letter, explaining that I had been called to see Mr. Clark[47]who was very ill at this place. Well, as he is very much better this afternoon, and I am allowed a few minutes respite, I propose entertaining myself for a little while at your expense.

Am afraid I am writing to you too often, but hope you will excuse it, as it is the most pleasant occupation I can engage in, and you must know I am very fond of indulging my <u>weaknesses</u>.

I left Beersheba in the rain and it continued to rain on me all the way – a distance of forty one miles over a much worse road than you have ever seen in your life or than I hope you will ever see. I got along very well, however, until I came to the descent of the mountain, and then alas! "I came to grief." The buggy was a very high one, and as it was pouring down rain I had the top up; in making a short turn where the road was fearfully steep, the buggy turned litterally (sic) bottom side up, and away I went: right out into a <u>mountain</u> <u>torrent</u>; fortunately the horse was too badly scared to run, and after getting out of the water I proceeded to take a <u>survey of the field</u>, and soon discovered that with the exception of being very wet and very muddy, and having a buggy spring smashed and the harness badly broken, <u>no</u> <u>damage</u> <u>was</u> <u>done</u>.

---

[46] Battle Creek place names do exist between Jasper and South Pittsburg, Tennessee.
[47] Richard Clark, an Englishman, is described in Isabel Howell's biography of John Armfield. Clark and two brothers had once been in the oil business with John D. Rockefeller who eventually bought them out. Richard invested in the stave factory (as shown in the letterhead Edward used for this letter) and a sawmill, and he was also the owner (though not the proprietor) of the Beersheba Springs Hotel along with three other cottages there.

Finally I patched up as best I could and proceeded on my journey a "wetter though a wiser man"; at about 9 o'clock P.M. I drew up in front of the Doty House and have <u>enjoyed</u>? the hospitalities of that institution ever since. Although I was completely chilled when I reached here last night, have suffered no inconvenience from it whatever. As I consider Clark out of danger for the present, will return to Beersheba tomorrow; and the prospects are good for another such ride as I had on yesterday, as it continues to rain as though it would never stop. Hoping to hear from you again soon, with kind regards to all I am devotedly

Yours
Ed N. Franklin.

Letter 7

Beersheba.
Septr 3rd/'71.

Miss Nannie.
 I am sitting in a darkened room, by Uncle Armfield's sick bed. He has been very sick for more than a week, and I fear he will never be up again. Seems to have let down completely, and there is nothing that will rouse him. He does not rally as he usually does, and talks a great deal about dying; has had his last resting place selected. I believe if he would just make up his mind to it, he could get up again, as there is no reason why he should die yet, but am afraid he will not do it.
 I have had the worst cold since my return from Jasper, I ever had in my life, which is not to be wondered at as I went and came in the rain. It rained on me all the way coming home, and I had another <u>turn</u> <u>over</u>. Have had but one <u>good</u> night sleep for a week; so with a wretched cold and loss of sleep I feel pretty well used up.
 Was a little disappointed that I did not hear from you last night. Wrote to your Father a day or two ago; and hope to get a <u>possitive</u> (sic) answer from him soon. Am coming to see you just as soon as I <u>can</u> possibly.
 With kind regards to all, I am

   Yours
      Ed N. Franklin.

Letter 8

Beersheba.
Septr. 9th/'71.

Miss Nannie.

Your letter bearing date of Septr 4th was gladly welcomed by your obliged friend, on last evening.

It were superfluous to add, that I was glad to hear from you; our associations in the past, our plans and prospects for the future, and the prompt answer I am giving your letter is sufficient guarantee to establish that fact beyond the shadow of a doubt.

That I am <u>dying</u> to see you, you well know: but am tied hand and foot. Uncle Armfield can't bear for me to be out of his sight for any length of time. My Father is coming up on Monday week — the 18th inst. and then I am coming to see you <u>right</u> <u>straight</u>. Will leave here Tuesday week — the 19th — and come directly to the <u>Empire</u> <u>Iron</u> <u>Works</u>.

And then I want you to tell me that you will marry me at the very earliest possible time; and we will go on to see <u>our</u> Sister in Maryland. If you write to me again before I see you — and I hope you will — tell me what you think of the <u>programme</u>? I don't think we can be married any too soon; what does my own Nannie think about it?

I can't contemplate the idea of being separated from one I love as I do you, any longer than is absolutely necessary, with any degree of patience whatever.

The sooner you <u>take</u> <u>charge</u> of me the better it will be for both of us, for you must know that every day I live by myself, (I have no Sister now) I am becoming more confirmed in my <u>bachelor</u> <u>habits</u>.

Only went in the ballroom once after the "ball" and then danced only one set, and have not been to church since you left. That is very <u>bad</u>, I know, but I have been very busy?

Dr. Winston and Miss Jennie left three or four days ago; in fact nearly everybody has left the hotel; only a few families of

<u>Yergers</u>,[48] remain "to tell the tale." Think they will stay until the 20th. Capt. Porter's[49], Mr. Brown's[50] and Maj. Banks'[51] families will be here, I suppose, until the first of October, and perhaps, later.

Thanks for the assurance that I can't write too often; for I love dearly to write to <u>you</u>.

Have not been well since my expedition on Battle Creek; still have a "bad cold" and dreadful cough, but think a trip to the <u>furnace</u>[52] will cure me entirely. Is your climate beneficial for <u>consumptives</u>?

We have a photographer here, and have been getting all kinds of pictures. More views than you could imagine <u>in a week</u>; and groups containing men, women, children, horses and carriages, dogs and everything in the world – <u>almost</u> – Will bring some down with me.[53]

Uncle A is a little better today. Aunt M is quite well. Present my kindest regards to all, and accept the best love of

        Yours truly
           Ed N. F.

(postscript)

I wish very much you would write Aunt M about this little affair of ours; am sure it would relieve her very much. Won't you do it for <u>my sake</u>? Remember, please, that your letters give me more pleasure than anything else <u>too</u>, and let me have another very soon.

        Ed N. F.

---

[48] Judge William Yerger (1816-1872) of Mississippi was one of these. He and his family have been at the resort all summer. He would die the next year, but other Yergers continued to visit for many years.
[49] See Letter 12 for a detailed reference on Capt. Porter and his wife.
[50] W. L. Brown of Nashville is listed as visiting Beersheba Springs that summer.
[51] Maj. A.D. Banks (d. 1881) from Mississippi had been an officer on General Joe Johnston's staff, had once been Postmaster of the House of Representatives, a correspondent for the Cincinnati Enquirer, and Stationery Keeper of the U.S. Senate. He is shown as having visited Beersheba Springs that summer.
[52] Edward uses the terms "Furnace" and "Iron Works" interchangeably, referencing Daniel Hillman's Kentucky home and business operations.
[53] Susan Snow of the Beersheba Springs Historical Society believes that a number of the photographs at the Beersheba Springs Museum originated from this photography session. Many were turned into slides for viewing in a stereopticon.

Letter 9

Please don't sign yourself my <u>friend</u> any more, for you are far dearer than any <u>friend</u> ever was. Coming from one I love as I do you, it sounds cold indeed. I don't wish to complain, <u>you know</u>.

Beersheba Springs.

Friday Septr 15th/'71

<u>My</u> <u>own</u> <u>Nannie</u>.

Now, does that sound very indifferent? How could you intimate such a thing, when you know – or ought to know very well – that I love you more than I do my very life? My soul is blended, – at least – it seeks to blend itself with thine.

Of course you are very, very much mistaken, and if you ever, as long as you live, ask me such a question, <u>on</u> <u>such a</u> <u>subject</u>, again, I don't know that I will ever forgive you. In fact I don't know that I ought to forgive it this time: but will just assume the position that you were not in earnest, and overlook it. How could I be indifferent to my heart's sweet home, my spirit's shrine?[54]

Why, my own love, you are the "beacon light"[55] *of my existence; you are a part of my life, my <u>everything</u>, and without you my life would be a blank, aye, worse than a blank, it would very soon resolve itself into <u>nothingness</u>. Now don't, for mercy's sake, ever insinuate anything pertaining to <u>indifference</u> again: but only tell me you love me as much as I do you, and I am satisfied. I believe you do love me – of course you do – but you know you have never yet <u>told</u> me so.*

If you did not love me, you would never have promised to become my wife; but I would never tire of hearing it, in so many

---

[54] In Letter 10 it is shown Nannie had accused Edward of being "indifferent." As to what is unclear. Considering he later refers to this his reply letter as 'silly', it does not appear to have been especially serious. Nevertheless, he reassures her in this letter with beautiful language.

[55] Though the meaning is clear, the reference is uncertain, but could be from a popular early 1800s poem by a Miss Pardoe, entitled "The Beacon Light."

words. I know, the three monosyllables, "I love you," coming from you, would be the sweetest music in the world.

Do you know you belong to me now? It is a <u>truism</u>, nevertheless, for I have received a letter from your Father, in which he gives me his <u>daughter</u>; so you see I have a right to call you "my own Nannie": haven't I dearest?, and mayn't I always call you so? and don't you love me more than everybody else in the world?

Please excuse my string of questions; and if this is the <u>silliest</u> letter you ever received in your life, why just forgive the writer, on the plea that he is too much in love to be <u>entirely sane</u>. I believe I told you once, that a <u>man</u> in love, had less sense than anybody, or anything in existence; and now, I have no doubt, you are almost, or quite ready to agree with me. I have never seen anything <u>sad</u> in the "lesson of loving"; am sure that is a mistaken idea, unless "love's young dream"[56] has been <u>particularly</u> kind to us. Don't you think ours has been <u>rather</u> pleasant than otherwise? So far, everything has worked just as I would have had it.

Your Father is certainly a very prompt man: and has attended to my case beautifully. Have thanked him by letter, and am more than anxious for an opportunity of doing so verbally.

Your letter from Shelbyville took me, a little, by surprise. I thought you only intended remaining there a few days, and have made arrangements to visit the Iron Works next week: but now scarcely know what to do about it. Wish you were <u>here</u>, to give me your advice.

However, I will go next week anyway, and see your Father and other relations; and then, <u>if you will let me</u>, will come on to Shelbyville to see you, and if you wish it, bring you back to the Iron Works – and, perhaps, if you are <u>right good</u>, up to Nashville.

Wrote you a <u>long</u> letter a few days ago, telling you of my plans, and asking your views in regard to them. Unless you are very bitterly opposed to it, I will insist that we be married this Fall – and just as early this Fall, as you like.

---

[56] A reference to a poem of that title by Thomas Moore (1779-1852), reproduced on page 18 in this book.

Please write to me immediately, on the receipt of this letter, and tell me if I shall come on to Shelbyville for you. Direct your communication to the Furnace as I shall leave here on Tuesday next, for that place. Thanks for the assurance that I shall receive a cordial welcome, though I am sorry you won't be there to welcome me.

Tell Grace,[57] I don't know that I can ever forgive her for taking you away, just at this time.

Had a letter from Sister a few evenings since. She "certainly" has not forgotten you, for she was complaining dreadfully of <u>your</u> not writing to <u>her</u>. It is a little singular that you should each be complaining of the other for the same offence; think if you would write without counting letters it would do away with all that sort of thing.

By the way, I don't think you have received all of my letters. With one exception, I have written to you two or three times every week since you left here,[58] and some of the letters, I know, were of a very <u>respectable</u> <u>length</u>. You should remember, I have a great many interruptions, and haven't as much time for letter writing, as my little sweetheart has.

My Uncle is still no better, and I very much fear he will never be up any more. He insists on being buried on the mountain; the place he had selected — I don't think you ever saw it — is what is called the ice-house garden, a very pretty spot up to the right of Mr. Bass's Cottage.[59]

My Father will be up on Monday next.

Be sure to write me a letter, to the Iron Works, as soon as you receive this.

---

[57] Grace was Nannie's younger sister and would have been 13 at the time. Eventually upon her marriage she was Grace Cora Hillman Scales. Grace Street running beside McFerrin Park in Nashville is named for her. In any event, it appears Grace is in Shelbyville, Kentucky, the location of her preparatory school, and Nannie is visiting her.

[58] That he admonishes Nannie and his sister for counting the letters they write to each other is quite humorous considering he himself is doing so.

[59] The Bass's cottage in Beersheba Springs, now referred to as Turner Cottage, is directly across the street from the Armfield home and right next to the Armfield Cemetery. John Meredith Bass (1804-1878), who built the cottage, was a friend of Armfield's.

The young ladies from "over the way" are over here every evening.[60]

With <u>all</u> my love, I am
Yours
Ed N. F.

---

[60] In Letter 16, Edward lists the names of some of these ladies, and they are almost certainly guests at the hotel, invited over to the house by Aunt Martha for socializing and doing needlework together.

Letter 10

Beersheba Springs.
Monday Septr 18th/'71.

My own Nannie.

I wrote you a letter day before yesterday telling you I would leave here tomorrow — Tuesday the 19th — for the Iron Works, and requesting you to direct your next letter to that place. This morning it is my painful duty to retract the whole thing. Uncle Armfield has grown worse suddenly, and I find I cannot leave here at present possibly; and what is worse, can't tell when I will be able to get off, probably not for a week or ten days.

What I wish now is for you to write to me at Beersheba, and tell me about how long you will be in Shelbyville; and if you are there when I leave here, I will come on there, and go with you to the Furnace, — that is — if you will allow any such proceeding. You know your Father has given you to me now; and there is no impropriety in my calling for you and taking you home. Do you think there would be any?

Please excuse me for altering my plans so very often; it is all, I assure you, attributable to the force of circumstances. Would not, for a world, have you think me <u>changable</u> (sic), for such is not the case. The heart, you have made forever your own, knows no change; it shall be true, and only yours, as long as there is a throb.

You distressed me greatly by insinuating that I had grown indifferent: but as I pretty well exhausted that subject in my letter of the 15th, will let the matter drop, hoping that you will not let your imagination lead you into any more such <u>grievous errors</u>.

The weather here now is perfectly charming — like "Indian Summer," and just cool enough to be delightfully pleasant. Nearly everyone from the Hotel has gone, and except for the presence of our old friend the Captain — Sheafe[61] <u>of course</u> — it would look desolate

---

[61] Capt. Charles A. Sheafe (born 1832-died sometime after 1909) was at the masquerade ball at Beersheba in August. He dressed as a "'Black Prince' dressed in black velvet spangled in silver."

indeed. Yes, he is actually here again; came up about a week since and will probably remain until the Hotel closes. I suppose you would not enjoy being here now, would you? with everybody gone except a few of us?

My cough still continues to be rather troublesome; though it could not well be otherwise, as I am up so much at night. I have had only one <u>good</u> night's sleep for three weeks, and begin to feel the effects of it very keenly.

Please write to me very soon my dear one, and believe me lovingly

        Yours.
        Ed N. Franklin.

Interestingly, in comparison to some of the other men mentioned, he was in the Union Army, having been a lawyer in Hillsboro, Ohio at the beginning of the war. He was in the 59th Ohio Regiment and fought at Shiloh and Stones River. Moving to Murfreesboro in 1865, he was elected a Congressman in 1868 but was not allowed to hold the seat in this Reconstruction era due to being a Democrat and opposition by the Republican governor. He continued with his lucrative law practice in Murfreesboro. He patented a fishing rod holder in 1890.

Letter 11

Beersheba.
Thursday Septr 21st/'71.

My own Love.

My dear Uncle is dead. He breathed his last at 12 o'clock last night. Earth can illy afford to lose such a man as he was, – truly one of nature's noblemen.[62]

I missed, more than I can tell you, the gentle ministrations of my dear Sister, during his illness. And he loved her with a love that was truly beautiful to see; he never mentioned her without shedding tears. It will shock her greatly.

I <u>cannot</u> write this morning, my dear one, but, you need no words to tell, how, more than life I love you.

Excuse me please, and <u>do</u> not attribute brevity to "indifference."

I will leave here on Sunday and go directly to the Works. Must see you just as soon as possible.

God bless you, Good-bye.

Devotedly Yours
Ed N. Franklin.

---

[62] The idea he is a nobleman can be understood as family sentiment. See the editor's essay entitled "Legacy" near the end of this book. Modern-day analysis looks upon John Armfield along with his business partner, Isaac Franklin (Edward's great uncle), as two notorious slave traders. Armfield's generosity in sundry causes following his years in the slave business is a fact, proving himself an enigmatic figure. Clearly, from Edward's point of view, this man had raised him from childhood and was dearer to him than his own father.

Letter 12

Beersheba.
Septr. 25th/'71

My own Love.

You see I am still at Beersheba. Have been necessarily compelled to change my programme a <u>third</u> time. Just as soon as I made known my intention of leaving here on yesterday, as I told you I would do, Mrs. Porter, who has another fine boy, <u>rebelled</u> and I was forced to promise to remain another week on the mountain to guard against any accident,[63] at the end of which time my Father will come up again to relieve me; and then I will immediately come to see you, <u>sure</u>. Yes, unless something <u>wonderful</u> transpires to prevent, I will leave Beersheba next Sunday and come directly to the Iron Works. Am afraid you will become completely disgusted with my very many appointments, but hope you understand fully the difficulties with which I have had to contend. And even now I don't know where you are; have not heard a word from you for a very long time. The last letter I had from you was written immediately on your arrival at Shelbyville: and don't know, consequently, whether you are still there or not; but will direct this to the furnace as I have already directed three to the former place. Are you never going to write to me anymore? This is the <u>fourth</u> letter I have written you since receiving one from yourself.

But you needn't write now, as I will leave here before your letter could possibly reach me.

---

[63] Capt. Alexander James Porter (1824-1880) and his wife were close to the family. He was a Confederate captain on the staffs of Gen. George Manly, Gen. John C. Brown, and Gen. Benjamin F. Cheatham, surrendering at Greensboro, NC. His second wife, referenced here, was Rebecca Greer Allison (1838-1922), and they did indeed have a child in 1871, named for his father. The captain's deceased first wife was Martha Watson who was distantly related to Nannie. Capt. Porter was the last Porter to live in Riverwood Mansion in Nashville, his ancestral home, before selling it to Judge Cooper in 1859. Indeed the first wife's ghost is believed to haunt Riverwood Mansion. The baby boy born in Beersheba, Alexander J. Porter, grew up in Nashville, worked for the Board of Parks Commissioners, married Minnie Bond, and had four children. He died in 1949.

Wrote you a very short letter a few days ago telling you of my dear Uncle's death. Although we had expected it for a long time, it was a great shock to us all. It does not seem at all like the same place. All the time after you went away I was in the habit of spending the evenings in his room; and since his death have been almost lost.

My Brother arrived here from the South this evening; did not bring his wife with him.[64] *Expect Sister and Geo(rge) Van Bibber the last of this week. Have not heard from them, but have written for them to come.*

Please make up your mind to be married just as soon as possible; would like so much for us all to be here together this Fall, if only for a few days.

Aunt Martha is quite well.

Present my regards to <u>all</u>, and accept all the love of

    Yours

        Ed N. F.

---

[64] Edward's elder brother was John Armfield Franklin. A four-year veteran of the war, he surrendered his arms at Appomattox. At the time of his eponymous uncle's death, he was employed as a traveling salesman for a whiskey company in Louisville, but despite what Edward believed, he was not married. His lover, Alice, was his traveling companion, though he passed her off to everyone as his wife. The truth became known some time later.

Letter 13

Beersheba.
Octo' 10th/'71.

My own Love.

    I have just reached here,[65] and my first thought is of you, and my first act (after eating a <u>light</u> supper, of course) shall be to write you a <u>short</u> letter; for I love you ever so much tonight, and if such a thing is possible, believe I love you more and more every hour. –but you will say this is all <u>foolishness</u>, so I will have done, and continue with something else.

    After a pleasant? drive, I reached Hopkinsville[66] on yesterday afternoon about a quarter after one o'clock. It was not <u>very</u> lonely after all, for you were with me – in thought – all the way, and really the ride seemed quite short. I met a gentleman about seven miles from Hopkinsville, at a very pretty little spring, who had no <u>lunch</u>; I opened mine and invited him to help me get through with it. He very <u>kindly</u> assented and we immediately <u>fell</u> <u>too</u> (sic), and I assure you enjoyed it hugely. I ate, and thought of my little "rose-bud," and he ate, and talked all the time of the Hopkinsville fair, the trotting races and a lot of things about which I cared nothing. After finishing the lunch and bidding Mr. I-don't-know-what-his-name-was an affectionate? good-bye, I continued my journey reaching H(opkinsville) at the time before mentioned. Spent the time there rather pleasantly loafing, until the train came along, then got aboard

---

[65] Since posting the previous letter, Edward had finally achieved his wish, and his duty, to visit Nannie and her father and family at the Empire Iron Works in Trigg County, Kentucky. He has now returned to Beersheba.

[66] Hopkinsville, Kentucky was the location of the train station he would have traveled to following his visit to the Works in Trigg County.

and was landed in the "Rock City"[67] about half past seven. Went round first thing and delivered your note and bundles to Nora.[68]

Saw a good many of our friends, and find they know more about our affairs than we do. Notwithstanding I was so confident that no one knew where I was, they all seemed to know perfectly well that I had been to see you, and that we were to be married early in November. It seems to be the talk of everyone, and in fact I am not surprised since I find that the gentleman to whom Gen. Bates[69] wrote in Gallatin is a son of Judge Joe Guild[70] of Nashville. They have a large connection and of course have talked it around generally. Hope you will <u>not</u> <u>be</u> <u>afraid</u> <u>to</u> <u>show</u> <u>yourself</u> <u>in</u> <u>Nashville</u> <u>after</u> <u>it</u> <u>all</u>!

Have only been here a few minutes, consequently don't know what is going on; haven't seen anybody except Pa and Aunt Martha. Found a letter here for me from Geo(rge) Van (Bibber) saying they would not be out. Sister said it would pain her too much to come just for so short a time. Will write you again in a day or two and tell you of our movements.

What do you think? Pa did not expect me at all; and says — when he found where I had gone, he didn't <u>know</u> that I <u>ever</u> <u>would</u> <u>come</u>. He is delighted with the prospect of having you for a daughter. Sends his love. You must excuse this letter, as he is talking to me all the time I am writing.

It grew so dark before I reached the foot of the mountain tonight that I could not see my horse; had to let him pick his own way. Please give my love to each member of your family.

With all the love I <u>can</u> <u>command</u>, I am

---

[67] Rock City was a nineteenth-century nickname for Nashville, and so the reference has nothing to do with the geologic wonder of the same name near Chattanooga that later became a favorite destination for travelers.

[68] Considering he does not apply "Miss" or "Mrs.," Nora is likely a servant, perhaps at the Hillman home in Nashville, to whom Nannie has sent some necessary items for the running of the household.

[69] Probably means General William B. Bate (1826-1905), a Sumner County native and Confederate General who later served as Governor of Tennessee from 1883-1887 and U.S. Senator from 1887-1905.

[70] Judge Josephus Conn Guild (1802-1883) was a Gallatin native. The son referenced here was likely Walter Josephus Guild (1843-1879), as according to Guild descendant, Cass Holly, he was the only son who was living in Gallatin at the time, at Rose Mont, the Guild home. Historic Rose Mont is now an events and wedding venue on South Water Street in Gallatin.

>   Yours always
>   Ed N. Franklin.

(Post script to the above, written the following day.)
>   Please write to me <u>very</u> <u>soon</u>. Have just written a short note
to Mrs. Hillman.[71]
>   Ed N. F.

Wednesday Morning.
>   *Octo 11th/'71.*

---

[71] In the next letter it is clarified he means Emily Gentry (Mrs. T. T.) Hillman.

Letter 14

Beersheba Springs,
Thursday. Octo. 12th/'71.

My own Love.
 Tonight Aunt Martha and I are all alone, and as I find she is more interested in a piece of work, she is engaged in, than she is in my affairs, I am determined to give my attention to what I am most interested in, and by way of carrying out my determination will devote the evening, or a part of it any way, to yourself.
 So now, I am ready quite, to turn my most devout attention to you — my heart's dear idol. And the very first thing that presents itself is a question: did you miss me very much after I had said "good-bye sweetheart"? as much as I did you? or did you think you would see me again so soon that it made no difference if we were separated for a while? I assure you, the separation of a day even is painful to me, for there is a vacancy <u>somewhere</u> (in my "heart of hearts," perhaps) that nothing but your presence can fill. Then dearest, you will not delay the consumation (sic) of our happiness, one day longer than is absolutely necessary, will you? but I know that you will not, and would not <u>hurry</u> you for the world — <u>if</u> <u>I</u> <u>could</u> <u>help</u> <u>it</u>.
 Except that it is uncomfortably <u>cool</u> up on the mountain the weather is perfectly splendid. It rained just enough on yesterday to lay the dust nicely, and today has been one of the brightest I ever enjoyed. We had some ice last night.
 The scenery from the "Sun-set rock" now is grand, sublime, and <u>everything</u> <u>else</u> you can imagine. I never saw anything like the varied tints the foliage on the mountain opposite has assumed; indeed, it is wonderful; language conveys but a poor conception of it. Never having been here so late in the fall, before, I never saw the mountain after it had been touched by <u>our</u> <u>friend</u> "Jack Frost," until

now[72]: but the evidences of his having paid his anual (sic) visit are self-evident. As it is getting so cold, I am urging Aunt M to let us get away just as soon as possible, and I think we will leave here in about ten days, or two weeks at farthest. She insists on staying as long as Capt. Porter's family does, and I think they will get off about that time.

The Capt. told his family when he came back, that our engagement was so generally known of in Nashville, that he might as well tell them; so they know all about it.

Aunt Martha says she is very sorry she can't see us married, but will be compelled to go on to Baltimore. Don't know when she will leave Nashville. I will write you before we go. Tell me if you know just when you will be in Nashville.

I wrote to both yourself and Mrs. T. T. Hillman the night I got home. Remember me kindly to all, and please write very soon.

>   I am devotedly
>   Yours
>   Ed N. Franklin.

---

[72] Considering boarding school education, it makes sense Edward would have been away from home during the autumn season. Also, the Armfields would usually winter in Louisiana and at least once in Florida (with the exception of during the Civil War when they remained in Beersheba), so possibly they would have left Beersheba for a winter-time residence by the time the leaves turned color.

Letter 15

Beersheba Springs.
Octo. 15th/'71.

My own Love.

Although I only mailed a letter to you on yesterday, I have a pretty good excuse for writing again today, in the fact that I was forced to mail the letter in Altamont, and have no confidence in that route. Think it very doubtful about your receiving it inside of a month or six weeks. The mail routes and post office department in this section of country has grown to be a decided nuisance — both public and private. It takes a letter two or three days to come here from McMinnville only, and we never get the Nashville papers under a week or ten days after they are issued; so you can form some idea of the irregularity with which the P.O. department is conducted after the season as Beersheba is closed. Don't think I will ever be <u>caught</u> here at this time of year any more. Considering the trouble at both ends of the mail route between us, am afraid our correspondence will prove very unsatisfactory as long as I remain here, but that will be only for a short time, fortunately, as we will leave on Tuesday week.

Aunt Martha insists that she can go to Baltimore[73] with only Matilda[74] and Harriett (both of whom she will take with her) as a <u>bodyguard</u>; but I will go as far as Cincinnati with her anyhow; and as there is no change of cars from there to Baltimore she can go the rest of the way alone very well. Geo(rge) Van Bibber or Mr. Archer[75] will meet her in Baltimore. Harriett is perfectly delighted at

---

[73] Aunt Martha, now her husband John Armfield has died, is going to live with her nieces' families, the Archers and the Van Bibbers, in Maryland.

[74] Matilda Franklin (1828-1878), was initially a slave belonging to Aunt Martha's father, John Franklin. Even after freedom came to her, she remained a loyal servant to Aunt Martha. Much research has been done on Matilda by Heather Adkins, on the staff at the Tennessee State Library and Archives.

[75] Stevenson Archer was the husband of Blanche, Edward and Adele's cousin. See pages 9-12 in the introduction. Archer and Van Bibber were related to one another as uncle and nephew, and were law partners. Van Bibber would have a long, illustrious career as lawyer and judge. Archer, on the other

the idea of going to live with her "Miss Dell,"[76] for whom she seems to have the greatest respect and admiration. She thinks there were never two beings created, to compare with her "Miss Nannie" and Miss "Dell"; I need scarcely add that I fully agree with her.

You must know that you are both very dear to me; and I am fully convinced that I can't love either of you a bit more than you deserve. God bless you both, and preserve you for my sake.

In my last letter I enclosed a letter to you from Sister. She was complaining dreadfully of your not writing to her. In my reply I told her you were raising the same complaint of her. Now, I can't afford to have you two falling out about letter writing, so I will just give you the same advice I did her, that — "stand not upon the order" of writing, but write at once,[77] regardless of what has gone before; if you will do that and quit counting letters, there will never be any trouble whatever. Just suppose I were to count letters with you, how often would you get a letter from me? At the present rates, not a very great many.

But without joking, I wish very much you would write to me a little oftener; I have written you as many letters in the last week, as you have ever written to me in your life all put together. Would not have you think I am complaining, my dear; only making a mild suggestion, for the mutual benefit of us both.

While I think of it, I will ask you to direct your letters, hereafter, to Nashville.

Aunt Martha will not be in Nashville any time, as she doesn't wish to see anyone there; and after I return from Cincinnati, will be there all the time.

Please keep me posted as to your movements. Will visit you while you are at your Aunt's,[78] as I suppose she would like to see

---

hand, would one day serve a prison sentence for embezzlement while serving as Maryland State Treasurer.
[76] Adele.
[77] "Stand not upon the order of your going, but go at once," is from Shakespeare's *Macbeth*, and basically the meaning is not to be concerned with formalities.
[78] This aunt of Nannie's is Mrs. T.T. Hillman as referenced in Letter 14. Emily Gentry Hillman was both Nannie's sister-in-law and aunt, as she was her brother Thomas Tennessee Hillman's wife, and her stepmother Mary Gentry Hillman's sister.

<u>what</u> <u>I</u> <u>look</u> <u>like</u>. But suppose I will see you in Nashville before you make that visit.

Capt. Porter and I were out shooting yesterday, and succeeded in killing a nice mess of birds apiece.[79] Tomorrow we are going down in the valley for a day's sport; and as Maj. Banks has promised to go with us, I am sure we will have lots of sport, even if we don't find the birds; we call it "Banks' benefit." Just imagine the Major trampping (sic) over field and meadow, gun in hand, looking for birds he knows full well I can't kill to save his life. He says, he is not accustomed to shooting on the wing, but is very anxious to try his hand this fall.

Aunt Martha sends love, and says she will write to you before she leaves Beersheba.

I know you have grown tired of this stupid letter, so I will <u>subside</u>.

Remember me kindly to all, and believe me

                Yours only
                        Ed N. F.

---

[79] Probably dove.

Letter 16

 *--Please excuse me if I come to you too often.*

Beersheba Springs
Thursday Octo' 19th/'71.

My own Love.

    I can't think of letting this, your birthday, pass by without writing you a letter of <u>congratulation</u>. Yes, I congratulate you on your having lived to see another birthday come round, <u>in</u> <u>a</u> <u>state</u> <u>of</u> "<u>single</u> <u>blessedness</u>," and I sincerely hope that it is the <u>last</u> that will visit you under the same circumstances. I hope that the next one that comes, will not find you as Miss Nannie Hillman.

    Have you thought of me today? and if so, have you thought "<u>seriously</u>" that, <u>perhaps</u>, before another day of like importance dawns upon you, you will be dearer and nearer to me than you are now? and that your term of "maiden meditation, fancy free," will have expired? These are very "serious questions," my dear, and you should weigh them well; and remember, please, that no matter how great the sacrifice you make for my sake is, I will always love you enough to over balance the whole of it. You know very well that my whole life shall be devoted to you; for <u>with</u> your love, I am everything; <u>without</u> it, nothing. Without you to live for I would not care to live. So you see you have grown to be a part of my very existence.

    Although the Allisons[80] know all about our engagement – at least, I have been told that they know it – they have never mentioned it to me in any way, but have been just as kind about it as possible; of course they will be as kind to you, so you <u>needn't</u> <u>be</u> <u>afraid</u> <u>of</u> <u>them</u>. The only thing that would make me suspect them of knowing – had I not been told – would be that they are so very loud in your praise

---

[80] The Allisons could be the parents of Capt. Porter's wife, Mrs. (Rebecca Greer Allison) Porter. They were definitely alive at the time and may have wanted to be near when Rebecca had her baby in Beersheba.

whenever I am about. They seem to think a great deal of "Nannie"; and of course, that makes me love them all the more. I know that they are among my very best friends; and I don't know a family anywhere that I think more of than I do of each one of them. But must not say any more on that subject or you will think that I have grown <u>enthusiastic</u>; "which" I would not do anything of the kind for a great deal.

Capt. Porter and I were disappointed in our hunt on Monday last, by the rain. But Miss Alethia,[81] Miss Jennie Allen[82] & the Misses Murphrey[83] came over, notwithstanding the rain, and spent the day. They had a little "sewing bee," and as they turned out pin-cusions (sic), "lilliputian slippers" etc. by the dozen, – <u>more or less</u> – I could not help thinking of my own love, far away, who I knew to be so fond of just such pretty work.

And for fear of keeping you from something of the kind now, I will bid you good-night.

Yours ever.
Ed N. Franklin.

---

[81] Alethea Allison, sometimes spelled Alethia or Alathea. In 1876, she married James Brown Craighead.
[82] Rebecca Allison Porter's mother had been an Allen, and Jennie Allen was probably related to her.
[83] At least one Miss Murfree attended the masquerade ball. It is virtually certain that these are Fanny Noailles Murfree and Mary Noailles Murfree. See group photograph on page 84. These two ladies never married. Mary would go on to become a famous author of fiction under the pen name, Charles Egbert Craddock, and it is a fact she would visit Beersheba in summers. The ladies were connected to Nannie's sister-in-law, Sallie Murfree Frazer Hillman, wife of her oldest brother, John "Hart" Hillman. The Murfrees descend from Col. Hardy Murfree, for whom Murfreesboro was named.

Letter 17

(Editor's note: At a point since his last posted letter on Oct. 19, Edward has left Beersheba Springs for Nashville and soon sets up an office in the city to practice medicine. These next two letters, the first a very short note, are dated the same. Which is first is uncertain, and possibly both were posted to Nannie at the same time.)

Miss Nannie.

Please accept my compliments together with some birds. I have just gotten here from S(aundersville)[84] and have not heard from Mrs. Ewing[85]. Hope she is enough better to enjoy a bird.

I will be compelled to go back to Gallatin this afternoon, but hope to be able to come down tonight, if so, I will do myself the pleasure of calling this evening. If I don't come, however, know that it was impossible for me to get back; and know for that my heart is with you wherever I am.

Yours fondly
Ed N. Franklin.

Nashville, Octo 30th/'71

---

[84] Saundersville train station was near Gallatin.
[85] Considering all the mentions in the next several letters, Edward certainly means Mrs. Ewin, rather than Mrs. Ewing. The editor has found other instances in his research in which people would mistakenly add the "g" to the end of the Ewin surname, even within family references. See the footnote on the Ewins in Letter 18.

Letter 18

Direct your letters to 167 Church St. if you please.
    Ed N. F.

Nashville.
Octo. 30th/'71.

My dearest love.
    I left Nashville this afternoon at 2.30 o'clock expecting to go to Cincinnati, but found before going far that Aunt Martha would not allow me to do anything of the kind. She said she had told you she would not let me go, and I found her true to her word. I went with her, however, as far as "Pilot Knob,"[86] saw her safely off with her baggage all checked to Baltimore, and then returned to Nashville after having made three trips over the L & N. R. R. in one day, completely tired out and feeling lonely indeed.
    I got my supper, and went around to Capt. Ewin's[87] immediately thereafter, without making any <u>preparations</u> whatever, expecting to spend a quite pleasant evening with my heart's idol – my own dear Nannie.
    Imagine my bitter disappointment at finding you had been called away: but I must admit that my sorrow at hearing of your Father's illness overbalanced my disappointment at not seeing you. Rest assured that you have my heart's deepest sympathy; and remember, please, that if there is anything in the world that I can do,

---

[86] Pilot Knob refers to a train stop on the L & N just north of Saundersville train station, but before reaching Gallatin. The station was named for a nearby prominent hill (today being eaten away by a gravel quarry). Nearby was the first Franklin home, named for the hill—that of Aunt Martha's grandfather (Edward's great-grandfather), James Franklin, and his wife Mary Lauderdale Franklin, who settled their land claim there in the 1780s. The home of Martha's parents, John and Elizabeth Rawlings Franklin, was also very close by. Aunt Martha certainly had relatives in this area with whom she could have spent a little time before continuing her trip to Baltimore.

[87] Capt. William G. Ewin (1842-1882) had his leg amputated after being wounded at the Battle of Kennesaw Mountain. His second wife, Mattie (Martha Jane) Hillman Ewin (1848-1926), mentioned in the next several letters as being seriously ill, was the daughter of George Washington Hillman, Daniel's brother, and his second wife Susan, therefore a first cousin to Nannie. They were living in Nashville. Capt. Ewin served as Davidson County Court Clerk. These letters and other family evidence seem to indicate Nannie and Mattie were particularly close.

it shall be done with pleasure, and I will consider it a special favor to be allowed to render any assistance in my power. I am yours <u>to command</u>, so please take advantage of it, and by so doing you will oblige one who lives but to love you.

Of course I can come down, and will do so whenever you wish me to. But I sincerely hope your Father is already very much better. I know you will be kind enough to write me immediately.

I had a very pleasant conversation with Capt. Ewin, and was glad to learn that Mrs. Ewin was improving. I know she misses sadly your kind and gentle ministrations; and hope you will be permitted — by the restored health of your Father — to return to her — and to <u>me</u> — very soon. I had anticipated so much pleasure in your society this fall. Your note, for which please accept very many thanks, was delivered promptly.

Am much obliged for your kind solicitude for my health; and promise to take care of it for your sake, if for nothing else. I have a very pleasant room at Mrs. Wharton's;[88] like it much better than I did the "Maxwell."[89]

With all my love, I am

      Yours always
         Ed N. Franklin.

---

[88] Mrs. Wharton is likely the wife of J. C. or W. H. Wharton. See letterhead used for Letter 25.
[89] Maxwell House Hotel.

Letter 19

Nashville.
Nov. 2nd/'71.

My own Love.

Each day since you left, I have been round to the Iron store[90] for intelligence from the furnace, and was more than repaid today by having Mr. Cha(rle)s Hillman[91] tell me that he had just received a dispatch saying your Father was better. I was beginning to feel very much concerned indeed, as he told me on yesterday he had been delerious (sic), and was no better. I sincerely hope, however, that he may now get well without any farther (sic) troble (sic). Please write to me just as soon as you can, conveniently, and let me know just how he is; for you know that, as a rule, telegraphic dispatches are the most unsatisfactory things imaginable. I wrote to you night before last telling you I could, and would, come down at any time you wished it, and I now repeat the same <u>assertion</u> accompanied by a request that if there is anything in the world that I can do, you will call on me without any hesitation whatever. I have opened an office, it is true, but that does not, by any means, prevent my going down at any time.

I am a pretty good nurse and if your Father is to be sick any length of time please let me come and help get him up again.

I received a dispatch from Geo(rge) Van Bibber this morning telling me of Aunt Martha's safe arrival. I was very much relieved, by it, indeed, for although I insisted on going with her and she would not let me, if anything had happened to her <u>they</u> would never have forgiven <u>me</u> for it.

---

[90] The Tennessee Iron Store, operated by Hillman, Bro. and Sons, was located at 52 and 54 North Market Street in Nashville. They received and sold processed iron and iron items from the Tennessee Rolling Works.

[91] Charles Ellis Hillman was another of Daniel Hillman's brothers, an uncle to Nannie thus, and involved in the Hillman family iron business. He was also on the Board of Directors at Third National Bank and at Nashville Commercial Insurance Company. He would soon sell out of his share in the family business and start his own, and the former Hillman, Bro. and Sons firm would be known as D. Hillman and Sons.

 I thought of all that beforehand and did everything I could to have her allow me to accompany her, but she said there was no necessity for it and I was not well, and put a possitive (sic) veto on it.

 I am <u>nearly</u> well, however, and think I will be entirely rid of my <u>continued</u> cold in a very short space of time.

 I rode around with Dr. Eve[92] this morning to see some patients, and he gave me an invitation to attend the Introductory Exercises in the medical department of the University of Nashville, tonight; but I thought of your injunction to take care of myself, and concluded to stay at home and write to you instead of going out.

 Direct your letters, hereafter, to #167 Church St. – With love, I am

    Yours
      Ed N. Franklin.

---

[92] Dr. Paul Fitzsimmons Eve during the war was Surgeon General of Tennessee, and after Nashville was occupied by the Union Army, went to Atlanta and took charge of the Gate City Hospital. He returned to Nashville after the war.

Letter 20

Nashville.
Nov 4th/'71

My own Love.

Not a word have I heard from you yet; but as I have only written to you <u>twice</u> this week, must write again this afternoon, if only to repeat what I know you are tired of hearing already, that is, that <u>I</u> <u>love</u> <u>you</u>. Now, are you not tired of that <u>worn</u> <u>out</u> sentence? and don't you wish I could get up something new? I know you are, and do, and so do I wish it: but it is the very first thing that pops in my head (or <u>heart</u> I should say) every time I commence to write to you. And that is not the worst of it; it excludes every other idea utterly, thereby rendering me incapable of writing you anything like an interesting letter. Isn't that a terrible state of affairs? I love to write to you above everybody in the world and yet, write you poorer letters than I do anybody.

And now, my dear, for fear of disgusting you, I don't <u>think</u> — I won't say possitively (sic) that I will not — I will write you another letter until I hear from you.

I was delighted to hear this morning that your Father was getting well.

How soon do you think you will return to Mrs. Ewin — and <u>to</u> <u>me</u>? Have not heard from Mrs. E today, but on yesterday she was improving. Hope you will come back very soon, as I know <u>she</u> <u>needs</u> <u>you</u>: of course I am <u>not</u> <u>a</u> <u>bit</u> <u>selfish</u> in wishing you to return.

Since opening my office a good many of my friends have called, I suppose, by way of encouragement. Judge Lea was around on yesterday and assured me I would do a very fine practice after a little while. He gave me every encouragement, and urged me to marry as soon as possible. I told him I would do so just as soon as I could find somebody that would be willing to <u>sacrifice</u> <u>herself</u>, whereupon he was very much amused.

I was at Mrs. Allison's a few days ago. They were all pretty well. Saw Miss Jennie Winston yesterday afternoon; said you and I were to be married next month, she knew possitively (sic). I understand she and Mr. Cheatham[93] are to be married soon.

Please write to me soon, and tell me all about yourself. Remember me to all, and believe me

Yours
Ed N. F.

---

[93] Edward's understanding appears to be confused. Miss Jennie Winston, the daughter of Dr. J. D. Winston, did indeed marry later that year on December 26, 1871, not to a Mr. Cheatham, but to a Mr. Joseph Woods Gordon, a merchant of Columbia, Tennessee. Sadly, Jennie died without children a few years after their marriage, and Mr. Gordon then married Beatrice Parker.

Letter 21

Nashville, Tenn.
Nov 6th/'71.

<u>My</u> <u>own</u> <u>Love</u>.

Although it is already quite late, as I was the happy recipient of two letters from yourself today, I <u>must</u> write you some sort of a letter tonight.

If you only knew <u>half</u> how much those two letters added to my existence today, you would feel fully repaid, I know, for the trouble of writing them. When I was congratulating myself on our correspondence being done away with, it was simply on account of the irregularity of the mails, and not that I objected to either writing to or receiving letters from you. Wherever there are only two or three mails a week there is necessarily some delay of mail matter, and that is what I was objecting to, <u>seriously</u>. But to know that I will get a letter from you, at some time, is a very great comfort I assure you.

The tone of your letter of the 3rd inst. was particularly gratifying to me. It is the very first one in which you have expressed yourself, apparently, without any reserve whatever; and it assured me that you care more for me than you would ever before acknowledge. Yes, I believe in <u>mutual</u> confidence before everything else, and fully agree with you, that where there is confidence there is no reason why we should not be happy and contented. Am glad that you feel that you can look to me, for comfort and consolation, in affliction, but pray God you may be spared <u>that</u> affliction (the loss of your Father) for many, many long years to come. Am delighted to know he is recovering and will soon be restored to perfect health again; but, in <u>our</u> joy and gladness we must not be unmindful of the sorrow and affliction of others. It pains me no little to inform you that Mrs. Ewin has grown worse again. She is by no means out of the danger; and this evening her case was considered desperate indeed. I don't wish you to say much about this, as it was told in confidence. Don't think Capt. Ewin is aware of her true condition, and I should not have told you, had you not requested me to do so.

I must explain to you how I came to tell Miss Janie[94] of our engagement. It was to keep a promise, made to her, long years ago that caused me to tell her. I promised her, before she was married and before I dreamed of such a thing, that if ever I became engaged to anybody, I would tell her all about it; so when you promised to be my wife, and I had obtained your Father's sanction of the same, I deemed it my duty to tell her of my good fortune, and did so, without having first obtained your consent, for which I beg your forgiveness now? Will you grant it, my love? but I know you cannot refuse me that, can you?

I told Uncle Armfield of it because I felt that it was due him, as he had always been as a Father to me, and took a great interest in everything concerning me. He was very much gratified, because he loved us both and wanted to see us happy; and, by the way, our affair was the last thing that he talked about before his death. He called me to him and told me not to let his being sick prevent my going to see you. I intended telling you of this before, but neglected to do so, from time to time.

Had a long walk with your Brother H(art)[95] this afternoon. He is the proudest man I ever saw in my life, and told me to tell you he had the finest boy <u>in the world</u>; was only a few hours old, and weighed ten pounds and a half. Says he would have written to you himself, but was very busy – <u>doing nothing</u>, as I suppose. He thinks you will all be up here soon.

Yes, it would have been perfectly charming, if we could have gone to Maryland as Aunt Martha did; but you ladies have so much <u>fixing</u> to do that it takes a long time to get ready for such a "serious" operation.

I will be the proudest man in the world when I can call you <u>my own little wife</u>; and it shall be my life long object to make you

---

[94] There is no reference anywhere of a Miss Janie, and despite the difference in the spelling, it is likely Edward means Jennie Winston, as she is referenced so much elsewhere.
[95] Nannie's oldest brother, John Hartwell Hillman, known as "Hart." His young family was still living near and had not yet moved to Pittsburgh. He was in business with his father.

happy. I don't want you to promise to go with Aunt M to Beersheba in the spring; for I know I will be entirely too selfish to give you up so soon as that.

Pa was down to see me today; asked after you, and wishes to be remembered.

A great many friends have called on me at my office; and as I had a patient this afternoon, feel very much encouraged. Please present my regards to all, write when you feel like it, and believe me

Yours
Ed N. F.

Letter 22

Nashville.
Nov. 8th/'71.

<u>My</u> <u>own</u> <u>Love</u>.
    "Hearts that <u>love</u> can never remain silent,"[96] and mine, being particularly blessed with a large stock of that <u>commodity</u>, insists on having a chat with the object of its love this evening, and I being naturally obliging, am disposed to oblige it, by indulging its weakness. After this <u>lengthy</u> preface I will proceed to tell you that, without your presence, Nashville is very rapidly growing <u>unbearably</u> (excuse me for manufacturing a word, I could not think of the one I wanted)[97] dull and stupid. Under ordinary circumstances, I think I could get along bravely, but with thinking of you all the time, wondering how long it will be before I will be blessed with a sight of you again, etc., etc., I find the time drags heavily on my hands.
    For the first few days, while I was tired and worn down, I stood it very well – in fact, rather enjoyed being alone, but now that I am rested, and almost rid of my cold, I begin to sigh for a congenial spirit to spend a quiet evening with, after a day's "dry" work in the office. I go to my office at half past eight in the morning, remain until one, then come home to dinner, go back at half past two and stay until five, then come home again, every day the same thing.
    Have never been so entirely alone in all my life. I miss the dear absent ones more and more every day; but you, my dearest love, can and will take the place of them all; yes, you are to fill the vacancy, and but for a knowledge of that fact, I would be perfectly miserable: as it is, I am more than content; at least, I <u>would</u> <u>be</u> if you were only here.

---

[96] The origin of this quote is uncertain.
[97] The word 'unbearably', common today, may not have been common then.

I saw your Brother H(art) this evening, and he requested me to tell you that his new boy is quite sick and he is very uneasy about him. Mrs. Hillman[98] is doing very well.

Am sorry to say, Mrs. Ewin is very little better. Her case is almost hopeless. It is very sad to know that she is in such a condition, and you have my heartfelt sympathy. Hope your Father continues to improve.

Wrote you on Monday night acknowledging the receipt of two letters. With much love, I am

Yours
Ed N. F.

---

[98] Hart's wife was Sallie Murfree Frazer Hillman, daughter of Henry S. Frazer and Elizabeth Maney Murfree. Her mother's family descended from Colonel Hardy Murfree for whom Murfreesboro, Tennessee was named.

Letter 23

Nashville.
Saturday Nov 11th/'71.

My dearest Nannie.

"*Disappointment sinks the heart of man*"!⁹⁹ *I don't know why I did so, but nevertheless, I had set my heart on having a letter from you this morning, and when it did not come, was disappointed. So much for expecting <u>too</u> much from a young lady. But, as I have a few leisure moments this morning, will devote them to yourself. Will return good for evil, remembering at the same time, that "it is more blessed to give than to receive."¹⁰⁰ To make my letter doubly acceptable, will give you a little piece of good news, to start with, viz: Mrs. Ewin was much better on yesterday than she has been for ten days past, and Dr. Maddin¹⁰¹ entertained hopes of her ultimate recovery. Have not heard from her this morning, but will do so before closing my letter. The Doctor promised to let me know just how she is this morning, and as he has not put in an appearance yet, will not close my letter until he does.*

I wrote to you two or three evenings ago telling you that Hart's baby was sick. I have not been able to see, or hear from him since, but suppose the boy is better, or I would have heard something of it.¹⁰²

I stop in at Cpt. Porter's nearly every evening on my way up to supper. They are always very pleasant, and glad to see me, and abuse me if I pass by two evenings in succession without stopping.

I succeeded in making Miss Alethia very indignant a few evenings ago. She was saying something that she would not do; and

---

⁹⁹ An old adage often used alone, but sometimes followed by the phrase, "but the renewal of hope brings consolation."
¹⁰⁰ Biblical quote.
¹⁰¹ Either Dr. John W. Maddin or his brother Dr. Thomas L. Maddin, both well-known doctors in Nashville at the time. The brothers died one week apart in 1908.
¹⁰² The baby recovered. This son of Hart and Sallie Hillman was named Henry Frazer Hillman (1871-1930).

I told her if she was my sweetheart she would do it, because I would have <u>her</u> <u>trained</u>, as I had all my sweet-hearts; whereupon she was very indignant, and said she just wished you could have heard me make that speech.

Dr. Maddin has just returned from Capt. Ewin's and says Mrs. Ewin is better than she has been since she has been sick. I assure you it gives <u>almost</u> as much pleasure to convey this intelligence as it will give you to receive it.

Miss Lizinka Elliston[103] sent me an invitation to her house, in the country, last evening, but as it was a very disagreeable evening, I remembered my promise to you in regard to my health, and sent her an apology for not going and stayed at home <u>like</u> <u>a</u> <u>good</u> <u>boy</u>. Hoping you are all well, I am

devotedly
Yours
Ed N. F.

---

[103] Lizinka Elliston was from a prominent Nashville family. She married Edward L. Buford in 1875, and they had several children. Lizinka died in the flu epidemic of 1918-1919.

Letter 24

Nashville.
Nov. 14th/'71

My dearest Love.

    I have to thank you for a very sweet letter received this morning. I know you would feel flattered if you knew how many times I have read the <u>aforesaid</u> letter, today. I always feel like a new man every time I hear from you, and if I love you too much, remember please, that it is <u>your own fault</u>. I loved you, it is true, a long time before you ever knew anything about it, but it was all your fault even then. But, forgive me for calling it a <u>fault</u>. I don't mean that at all, but simply that you are the <u>innocent cause</u> of my being so much in love that I can do nothing, scarcely, but think of, and worship the object of that love.

    I thank you for the assurance that you will never tire of hearing of my love; and you may rest assured that I will always love you, and you only, as long as life lasts; and just as much "'mid the falling leaves, as I did 'mid the bloom of May."[104]

    I know you will forgive me for alluding to something that was not pleasant to you, when I promise not to do so anymore. I don't remember how I alluded to it now, but am sure it must have been inadvertently. 'Twas not with "<u>malice aforethought</u>"[105] I assure you. Of course I do not hold you responsible for that speech, any more than I do for a good many more made about the same time.

    Have heard you make several remarks, which, if I had thought, were your real sentiments, would have <u>scared</u> me off long ago. But I believed at the time, that you did not know yourself as well as I knew you. That sounds a little presumptious (sic) does it not? Forgive me. I loved you all the time anyhow, even when I thought you were saying things just to drive me off.

---

[104] From the poem, "A Woman's Question," by Elizabeth Barrett Browning (1806-1861).
[105] An old legal term meaning with malicious intent or with premeditation.

We have had a regular snow storm, which lasted until late this afternoon, and it has been as disagreeable and sloppy as possible all day, and this evening it has turned very cold. Have not heard from Mrs. E this today, but at the last accounts she was doing well, better than she had been since she was taken sick. Wrote you about her in my last letter. By the way, this is the seventh letter I have written; so you can tell if you have received them all. Have received all of yours save one written since you returned to the "Works" and one written before I left B(eersheba).

Had a letter from Aunt M this afternoon. All well. Sister wrote to you a few days before. With kind regards to all, and love to you

I am devotedly

Yours

Ed N. F.

Some company came in tonight, which caused me to wind up this letter rather hastily. Hope to see you early next week.

E.N.F.

Letter 25

<small>Office of</small> **J. C. & W. H. Wharton,**
<small>DEALERS IN</small>
DRUGS AND MEDICINES,
<small>ICE CREAM SODA WATER, SUPERIOR CHEWING BALSAM IN STICKS, &c.</small>
No. 38 UNION STREET.

Nashville, Tenn., <u>Nov 16th 187</u>1

God bless you, I would love to see you but can't. Am suffering from the severest calamity that ever befell me. Have just heard of the death of my idolized brother.[106] *Am on my way to the depot. Please excuse me, for I scarcely know what I am writing. Will see you tomorrow or the next day. Until then fare-well. Love me as*

Your own.
Ed N. F.

P.S.

Have told Mr. Wharton <u>all</u>.

---

[106] Edward's brother, John Armfield Franklin, died that very day, November 16, in Tallahassee, Florida. A telegram was received. According to an obituary, he died of a "short but violent attack of pneumonia," a sad, anticlimactic ending for a young man who survived the horrors of over four years as a very dedicated Confederate soldier. His paramour, Alice, was with him when he died. His premature death and late-discovered will would years later have a profoundly negative impact on the relationship between Edward and their father, Dr. John Washington Franklin, as described in the Afterword and Appendix 1.

Letter 26

Social Circle. Ga.
Nov. 21st/'71.

<u>My</u> <u>dearest</u> <u>Love</u>.

  I was so very unfortunate as to miss a connection last night, and was forced to remain at this miserable little <u>so</u> <u>called</u> "Social Circle"[107]*; if there ever was a misnomer that is certainly one, for I have tried it now since 8 o'clock last night, and am destined to keep on trying it until 10½ o'clock this morning, at which time my train is due; and so far from being anything like a <u>Social</u> <u>Circle</u>, it is very <u>squarely</u> <u>uncomfortable</u>. Am ready, quite, to exclaim, "Oh! Solitude where are the charms that Sages have found in they face, Better dwell in the midst of alarms, than reign in this horrible place."*[108] *To add to the disagreeableness of the place, it has commenced to rain this morning, and everything is dark and gloomy generally. Under such a combination of misfortunes, you see I turn to you for comfort, and already I have found it. To know that there is one, who loves me as I believe you do, and who I am allowed to love as much as my poor heart can love; is enough to cheer me even in my very darkest hours: yes, <u>more</u> <u>than</u> <u>sufficient</u> to compensate for everything else.*

  My detention here, will probably delay my return, but I still hope to see you Friday evening.

  Until last night, I had made beautiful connections, and the trip had not been at all fatiguing. Had company nearly all the way.

  And now, my Love, until I can see you again, will say good-bye.

    Love me as
      Your--------

---

[107] The body of his brother is being transported from Tallahassee, Florida to Gallatin, Tennessee for burial. Edward is going to meet the body and take possession of his brother's personal effects in Washington, Georgia. Social Circle, Georgia, is on the way.
[108] Line from "The Solitude of Alexander Selkirk," by William Cowper (1731-1800).

Ed N. Franklin.

P.S.
Will reach Washington[109] today.

---

[109] Washington, Georgia.

Letter 27

LOUISVILLE HOTEL

M. KEAN & Co.

Louisville, Ky.

Dec 14th, 1871.

<u>My own Love</u>.

"Mine to the core of my heart, my beauty!
Mine – all mine, and for <u>love</u>, not <u>duty</u>;
Love given willingly, full and free,
Love for love's sake, as I love thee."[110]

Excuse me please, for being <u>just a little</u> sentimental. How am I to help it, under the circumstances?

This is the first moment I have had time for anything outside of business since my arrival in Louisville;[111] and now my mind is so full of you that I can think of nothing else: but I must check it a little, as I am not quite through yet.

Will finish up everything this evening, and leave here at 11 ½ o'clock tonight. Shall stop in Sumner,[112] as I told you I would, and have a day's hunt, and <u>try</u> to be with you again on Saturday evening next.

The weather being favorable, Capt. Porter will meet me at Saundersville[113] on Friday morning. We will go to my Father's[114] to breakfast, hunt all day in the neighborhood, stay there that night,

---

[110] From the poem "Plighted," by Dinah Maria Muloch (1826-1887).

[111] Since John Armfield Franklin was employed by a Louisville company, Edward may have traveled there in order to take possession of any additional personal effects and to handle other business arising from the death of his brother.

[112] Sumner County, Tennessee.

[113] Saundersville train station on the L & N is close to Franklin family lands in Sumner County. Saundersville has today been absorbed by Hendersonville, though there are many Saundersville place names there still.

[114] As mentioned before, his father John Washington Franklin's home was "Oakley," a brick Gothic-revival mansion and farm on Nashville Pike near Gallatin.

take a <u>small</u> hunt again Saturday morning, and take the afternoon train for Nashville. How is that for a programme?

Will bring Mrs. Ewin some birds <u>if</u> <u>we</u> <u>have</u> <u>any</u> <u>luck</u>.

I have heard nothing of that letter you were to write me, and very much fear it will be reported among the <u>missing</u>. Of course, I know you have written it.

Except a little delay at Franklin, Kentucky, on account of the down train having run off the track ahead of us; my trip so far, has been devoid of incident or accident. Think, however, we will be able to get up something exciting tonight, as the train will run <u>against</u> <u>time</u> between here and Gallatin – <u>don't</u> <u>be</u> <u>alarmed</u>?

What do you think? I had some young lady visitors at my office the morning I left Nashville. Guess who. I know you can't guess, and don't think I will tell you.

And now, I know my own Nannie will pardon this stupid note, on the plea that I am very tired and almost worn out. I might say: "I am tired and sleepy too," and consequently "not in a condition to perform well."

Assuring you that you are far dearer to me than everything else in the world, I will sign myself

Yours always
Ed N. Franklin.

Afterword

To Greig's Bakery and Confectionary on Union Street in Nashville the order was sent by Nannie's stepmother, Mary Gentry Hillman:

1 Large Lady Cake with Raisins. Basket in Center, Gold Leaves, Hexigon Shape.
1 Large Dark Fruit Cake, Thick through, Round Mould.
1 Large Lady Cake with Citron Basket in Center, Silver Leaves, Hexigon Shape.
1 Lady Cake Large. Pure White. Handsomly-ornamented, Thick and Round Mould.
1 Large White Mountain Cake, square.
1 Large Jelly Cake, square, Elegantly Ornamented.
Ornamenting 1 Brides Cake, Temple raised work with Bridal Figure, pure White Ornaments.
5 lbs Fine Cakes, 2 lbs Egg Kisses, white, 4 lbs Fine French Candy, 2 Bowls Charlotte Rousse, 2 lbs French Crystalized Fruits, 2 Bowls Ambrosia, 3 lbs Mix Nuts. 1 Crystalized Orange Pyramid Temple, 1 Bowl Pyramid, New Style. 2 Dz. Large Oranges, 6 lbs Malaga Grapes, 3 Dz. Bananas, 2 Dz. California Pears. 1 Spice Round, 6 Beef Tongues, 6 Loaves Bread, 6 lbs Serated Crackers, 4 lbs Gold Popping Kisses, 1 lb Cocoa Candy, 1 lb Cream Chocolate Drops, ¼ Box Raisins, ½ Drum Figs, 2 lb French Prunes, 2 Gallons Amber Jelly, 5 lbs Cheese.

That was just from Greig's. An additional list indicates more was acquired elsewhere for the "Meat Table" to go with the spice round and beef tongues:

1 Whole Roast pig.
4 Turkeys for Chicken salad.
4 Ducks.
Sardines.
2 Turkey Large Sandwiches.
1 ½ doz. Birds.

Venison Saddle.
Pickles
Celery
13 cans Stewed Oysters.
5 cans Fried Oysters.
4 cans Raw Oysters.
Oyster Crackers

On January 3, 1872, three weeks after the last letter was written, Edward and Nannie were married at the Hillman home in Nashville.[115] Based on the tantalizing menu, it was a grand affair. In addition is a long, dowry-like list of all the furniture, paintings, silver, and other gifts given by Daniel Hillman to his daughter in order for her to later set up housekeeping. John Washington Franklin assuredly attended his son's wedding. Still in existence is one gift he presented his new daughter-in-law Nannie—a silver-plated cake dish engraved from him to her. This is currently in the possession of Kenneth Thomson of Gallatin, a Franklin relative and local historian.

Based on information found in the Nashville City Directories of the 1870s, for the years 1872 and 1873, Edward's name shows him as a physician with an office on Church Street and then at a different location in 1875. Their residence is the same as that of Nannie's parents, and it appears they lived there until 1878. Interestingly, for the year 1874, and from 1876-1878, Edward is not shown as a physician but rather as a salesman at the Hillman family's iron store on North Market Street. On a separate list of all Nashville physicians in each of the Directories, Edward's name is not shown at all. All of this information would imply he had some difficulty establishing his medical practice, or at the least he worked some of the time for Nannie's father and brothers. There was a nationwide economic depression in the 1870s which may have been an influencing factor. By 1879 at the latest they had moved to Mitchellville in north Sumner County on the L & N. It seems unlikely Edward could sustain a lucrative practice in that location, either, and perhaps he commuted on

---

[115] The home belonging to Daniel and Mary Gentry Hillman on McLemore Street in Nashville is described in the photograph section. Edward and Nannie were married by the Rev. W. J. Ellis, rector of Christ Church (Episcopal), Nashville.

the train into Nashville each day to work. During this decade four children were born to them: Florida (1872), Grace (1874), and Daniel Hillman (1876, called "Hillman"), all born in Nashville, and Edward Noel, Jr., (1879), born in Mitchellville.

Late in 1881, the family moved permanently to Gallatin, and the doctor established an office in Montgomery & Knight, a drugstore on the city square. Edward continued as a practicing physician the rest of his life, was a member of various medical organizations, and advertised his services. Another daughter, Nannie Marable, was born to them in 1884. This was followed, however, by two tragedies when, late that same year, five-year-old Edward, Jr., died, and the next year "Little Nannie" too passed on at only 22 months. Nannie's father, Daniel Hillman, also died in 1885,[116] and so, taken altogether, it was a difficult time for the family. Yet, they did buy a nice home that year on North Water Avenue where they would remain for the rest of their lives. It would have been in this house, named "Lone Pine," that in 1886 the sixth and last of their children was born—Charles Hillman, known as "Charlie." Thankfully, he proved to be healthy, and along with Florida, Grace, and Hillman, grew to adulthood. The family attended Emmanuel Church in Gallatin, an Episcopal mission established in 1881. This small church was located on East Main Street. Little Nannie was baptized here and likely Charlie was, too.[117]

At a point in the late 1880s, Edward became entangled with his own father, Dr. John Washington Franklin, in a lawsuit over the estate of Edward's deceased older brother, John Armfield Franklin. Upon finding his brother's will by chance hidden in an old gun box that Edward had received at the time of John Armfield Franklin's death, it was shown that his brother wished Edward to have his

---

[116] Daniel Hillman's final years were nothing like his early days prior to and just after the war, when he was riding high. In the latter 1870s he expressed to Nannie in letters fears of bankruptcy as his industry no longer produced as it once did, in part likely as a result of the 1870's depression. By the end of his life he had succumbed to melancholia, dying in the Kentucky Insane Asylum in Hopkinsville. Mary Gentry Hillman, his second wife, survived him another 23 years.

[117] Emmanuel Episcopal Church was disbanded in 1919, and the building torn down a few years later. An Episcopal Church presence would not return to Gallatin until 1956 when Church of Our Saviour was established. Nannie would have still been alive when Emmanuel disbanded. The families of her two daughters' husbands, the Andersons and the Houses, were members at Southern Methodist Episcopal Church (now First United Methodist Church), and possibly Nannie's spiritual needs were provided through that church in the last years of her life.

twenty-percent share of their Uncle John Armfield's estate. The brother had of course never received this share, since he had died only a couple of months after Armfield himself. Also in the will, John Armfield Franklin instructed Edward to buy the paramour "Alice" a train ticket to Louisville and to give her $500! Their father, John Washington, executor of the Armfield estate, refused to acknowledge the validity of this will. The bulk of the estate had of course been executed years before. John Washington accused his son of forgery; Edward sued his father. The extraordinary case, celebrated in the papers, advanced all the way to the Tennessee Supreme Court. There are voluminous records on it in the Sumner County Archives. Needless to say, son and father became estranged. Edward continued to gain advantage with each verdict, and the will was ultimately deemed valid. Yet the Supreme Court then put a serious check on it, determining that the statute of limitations prevented Edward from receiving anything from the original estate. However, some additional money had later come into the Armfield estate, and that later money was within the statute of limitations, and the court determined he was entitled to his brother's share of that money. This amounted only to $1890 plus some interest, and considering all the court costs, lawyers' fees, and the effect on Franklin family relationships, it was surely not worth the drama. Years later, their daughter Florida told Franklin relative Kenneth Thomson that the lawsuit was a big mistake and should never have happened.[118]

    Tracing the family forward (refer to Chart C on page 78), Edward and Nannie's first daughter, Florida, married Walter Leake Anderson, a local insurance salesman, and as a wedding gift Nannie bought for them the house next door to Lone Pine where they lived for many long years.[119] Florida is still remembered by older Gallatin folk as a devout Christian and Sunday School teacher. The Andersons had three daughters, but the first one, Nannie Hillman Anderson, rather like "Little Nannie" of a generation before, died before her second birthday. However, the other two Anderson daughters lived full lives.

---

[118] See Appendix 1 for a selection of articles and the Supreme Court report relating to the *Franklin v. Franklin* case.
[119] No doubt Edward's income by this time was a good one, but the basis of the family's wealth was in Nannie's investments in her Hillman brothers' enterprises.

The older, Sara McFerrin (known as Sara Mac) married Walton Maxey Jarman, one of the founders of Genesco, Inc., and there are many Jarman descendants in Nashville and elsewhere. The younger daughter, Grace Adele, never married. She lived most of her life in Gallatin, a bubbly and fun individual who was well-liked by everyone in town who knew her. Many of the Andersons are buried in the Gallatin City Cemetery.

Edward and Nannie's second daughter, Grace, married Allen Luke Palmer House of the prominent House family of Gallatin. Very sadly he died of typhoid soon thereafter, just before their only child, a daughter, was born. Allen Palmer House was named in memory of this father whom she never knew. Grace never married again, but returned with the baby to Lone Pine, remaining there the rest of her life, next door to her sister Florida. In addition to founding and serving as first regent of the General Jethro Sumner Chapter of the D.A.R., Grace was a wonderful artist, and many painted china pieces and framed art exist in the family today. Grace, having inherited Lone Pine, was the one who retained possession of Edward's letters. She is buried beside her parents at Mt. Olivet Cemetery in Nashville. In time, Grace's only child, Allen Palmer, married Oscar Eugene Martin, and there are members of this family in Gallatin to this day. Though the Martins inherited Lone Pine, the house was eventually sold and torn down to make room for Gallatin Nursing Home. However, Florida's house next door, "Maple Summit," is still a private home.

"Hillman" was the eldest son of Edward and Nannie. He attended Webb boarding school in Bell Buckle, Tennessee, and three letters exist that he wrote home during his time there. Sadly, his story, at least towards the end of his life, was not a happy one. He did at some point take a job with the L & N Railroad and worked as a station agent for several years at Gallatin. In 1904, at 28 years old, he died in Memphis. The first article in the local paper announcing his death indicated he had been one of the most popular boys growing up in Gallatin, and that as an adult he had been an excellent and professional employee. In a subsequent notice, the tragedy behind Hillman's death was made clearer. He had traveled to Memphis in order to undergo a course at a sanitarium due to drug addiction. Yet shortly upon completing the course, he overdosed on morphine at the hotel where

Reference Chart C.
Children and Grandchildren of Edward and Nannie

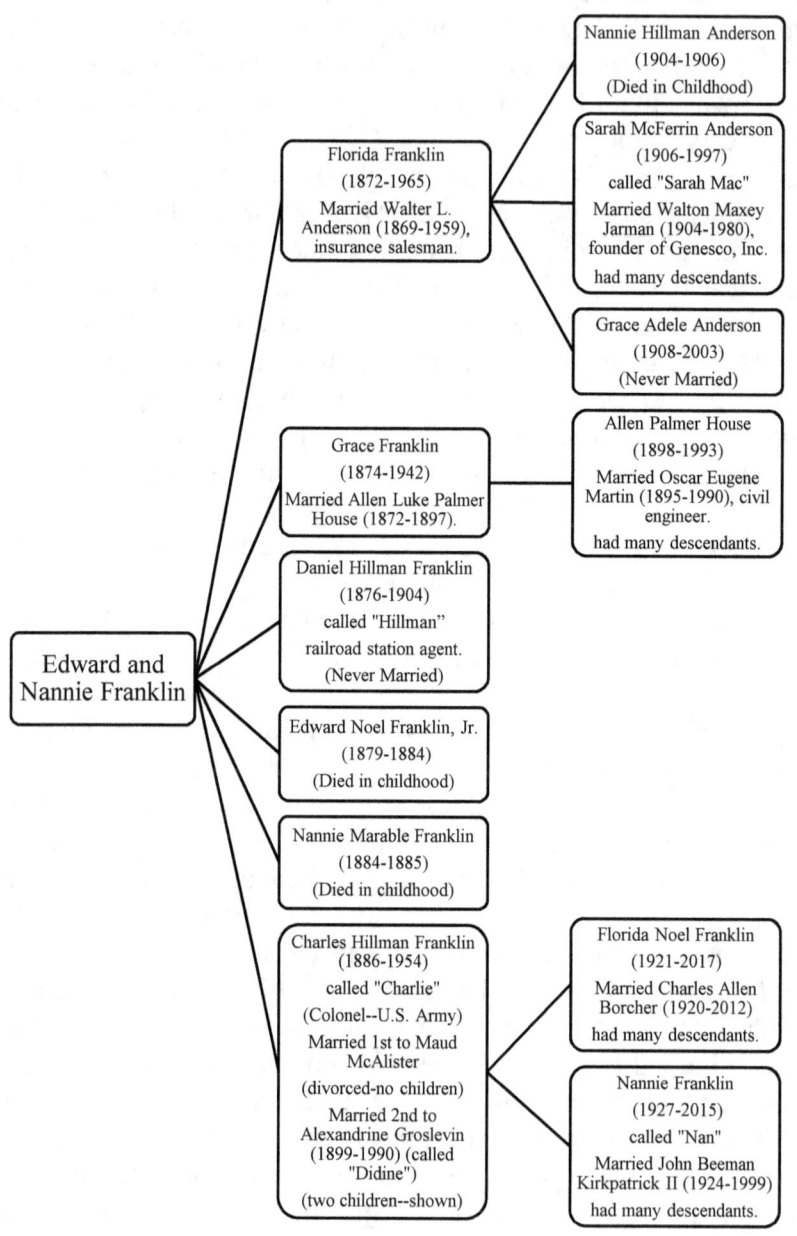

he was staying. Taken to a hospital, he did not revive. An unregistered stranger with him at the hotel at the time of the incident abruptly disappeared, and though searched for by the police, he was not seen again. Never married, Hillman's body was brought to Nashville, and he was buried at Mt. Olivet Cemetery.

Charlie was the last child born to Edward and Nannie. He first married, but then soon divorced, a woman by the name of Maud McAlister. Serving in World War I, he met a young French woman by the name of Alexandrine Groslevin, known as Didine. This second marriage proved life-long, and with Didine he had two daughters. The first, Florida, married Charles Allen Borcher. The second, Nan, named for her grandmother, married John Beeman Kirkpatrick II. There are many Borcher and Kirkpatrick descendants. Charlie had a military career, reaching the rank of colonel, and is buried at Arlington National Cemetery.

There are still Franklins in Sumner County descending from patriarch James Franklin who settled his Pilot Knob claim back in the 1780s. Yet the Franklin surname from Edward's branch died out with Charlie. However, the old family names continue to resurface as first or middle names in the family tree, including Franklin, Noel, Nannie, Adele, Hillman, Grace, and Florida. And there are many descendants of Edward's many half-siblings from his father's second wife, Sarah Baber, including the Franklins and Hoyts of Nashville. Some of these last share a historic vacation home in Beersheba Springs today.

Dr. Edward Noel Franklin died in Gallatin, November 21, 1909. As indicated, daughter Grace and granddaughter Allen Palmer continued to live with Nannie at Lone Pine—the Andersons next door were also ever present—until her death on October 6, 1923. Edward and Nannie are buried side by side with four of their children at Mt. Olivet in Nashville, not far from the grandiose Hillman monuments and Adelicia Franklin Acklen Cheatham's fabulous family vault. Allen Palmer's grandson, the editor of these letters, remembers his grandmother talking very fondly of her "Granny" to whom she was very close. The massive 1867 painting in its ornate golden frame of a beautiful, young Nannie which hung prominently in Allen Palmer's home was ever a source of childhood wonder, an instigator of questions, and by this last, an influence on the editor's love of history.

Photographs

Grace Huston Haines Hillman (1773-1826) and Daniel Hillman (Sr.) (1782-1831), of New Jersey. This Daniel was the first Hillman to make his way to the South. Opening a bloomery forge in 1830 on Roupes Creek, later Tannehill, he foreshadowed the eventual rise of nearby Birmingham as a center of iron and steel. He died less than two years later, but his sons, Daniel, Jr., Charles, and George, would soon follow his lead, landing themselves in Tennessee and Kentucky. They would expand enormously on the family's success in iron. Daniel, Sr.'s role in industry is interpreted at The Iron and Steel Museum of Alabama at Tannehill Ironworks Historical State Park. (Digitally remastered photocopy images. Original silhouettes—paper over black taffeta. Copies provided by descendant Grace Paine Terzian.)

Daniel Hillman (Jr.) (February 3, 1807—January 3, 1885). Born to Daniel Hillman and Grace Haines Hillman of New Jersey, his forebears had long been in the iron business. Establishing works in Tennessee and Kentucky, on the eve of war in 1860 he had 376 slaves working for him in Lyon and Trigg County. (376 is a minimal number, and some older secondary sources indicate hundreds more.) Called the "Iron King," at a point after the war his enterprises supplied 80% of all the iron produced in the South. (Hand-colored original portrait in the Family History Collection of Terry Martin. Photo reproduction by Aaron Thomas. Image size 14 X 17.)

Ann Jones Marable Hillman (February 17, 1818—April 2, 1862). Born in Montgomery County, Tennessee at "Escape" (no longer standing), home of her parents Dr. John Hartwell Marable and Ann Jones Watson Marable, her father served in Congress from 1825 to 1829. In this vintage photo of an original crayon-style photographic portrait she wears a pin depicting her husband, Daniel Hillman. She is buried in the Marable family cemetery in Clarksville. (Vintage photo of an antique crayon portrait. Photo in the Family History Collection of Terry Martin.)

The Marable Tapestry. Originally designed and executed in fine cross-stitch by Ann Jones Marable Hillman, this exquisite piece depicts the names of her Marable and Watson ancestors, husband, and also prominent politicians, perhaps well-known to her Congressman father, including Martin Van Buren, William Henry Harrison, John C. Calhoun, and Henry Clay. Ann died before completing it. (Original Cross-stitch, 1840s-1862. 80 X 33. In possession of the Martin and Halbrooks families. Rugby, Tennessee. Editor's image.)

Inset image of the Marable Tapestry. Names depicted in this inset are Ann J(ones) Marable, maker of the tapestry, D(aniel) Hillman, her husband, J(ohn) H(artwell) Marable, her congressman father, and two political giants, Henry Clay and J(ohn) C. Calhoun. (Editor's image.)

Nannie Hillman (October 19, 1847—August 6, 1923). Nannie was her nickname, though no one called her "Ann Fredonia." The beloved recipient of Edward Noel Franklin's letters was the older daughter of Daniel Hillman and Ann Jones Marable Hillman. She was born in Clarksville, died in Gallatin, and is buried at Mt. Olivet Cemetery in Nashville. (Artist, Samuel Bell Waugh. 1867 oil on canvas in the possession of Thomas D. Martin, Gallatin. Image dimensions 48 X 40, Frame Dimensions 62 X 53. Image from the Tennessee Portrait Project website.)

An invitation to Nannie to attend a "Grand Hop," in Honor of Ex-President Andrew Johnson at Overton Hotel in spring of 1869. "Overton's Hotel" and "Overton's Folly" were early names of the edifice opened officially in the fall of 1869 as the Maxwell House Hotel. It was used for years prior to its official opening. (Invitation in the Family History Collection of Terry Martin.)

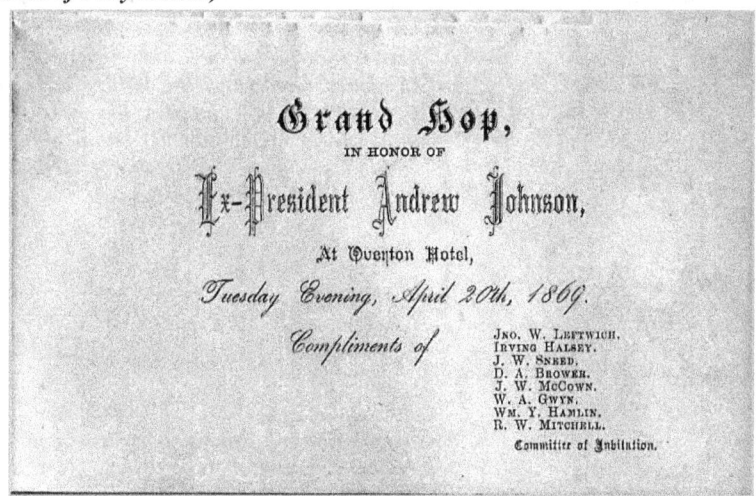

This image above, labeled "The Combination," was taken in Philadelphia, January 2, 1866. Nannie, 18 at the time, is on the far left, her cousin Mattie (Martha Hillman, later Mrs. Ewin from Edward's letters) is sitting lower right with dog in lap. The others' names are listed as Fannie Murfree, Mary Murfree, Eugenia Marshall, Mary Westcott, Louis Allen and Charles Westcott. The Murfree girls are assuredly the ones mentioned in Edward's letters as having visited Beersheba, as they are known to have spent much time there. Like Nannie and Mattie, they also attended Chegaray Institute, a French boarding school in Philadelphia. Possibly all the girls in the photo were students there. Mary Murfree would one day become a famed author under the pen name, Charles Egbert Craddock, a key figure in the development of Appalachian fiction. One key Craddock researcher, Dr. William Hardwig of the University of Tennessee, identifies Mary as the one seated left, and sister Fannie standing in white coat, right of center. (Original image in the possession of Thomas D. Martin.)

A stylish young Nannie. (Original image in the Family History Collection of Terry Martin.)

The two sons of Daniel Hillman and Ann Jones Marable Hillman were John Hartwell Hillman (left) and Thomas Tennessee Hillman (right). They were helping operate their father's business at the time their sister Nannie was receiving letters from Edward in 1871. Talented and driven, each would one day have his own industrial empire, one in Pittsburgh and the other in Birmingham.

John Hartwell Hillman, Daniel Hillman, Nannie Hillman. This (right) depicts Nannie with her father and her oldest brother, John Hartwell Hillman (September 27, 1841—October 10, 1911). Known as "Hart," he married Sallie Murfree Frazer and eventually moved to Pittsburgh. They have many descendants. Founder of Hillman Coal and Coke Company, today's Calgon Carbon and The Hillman Company are descendent businesses. (Vintage photos above and right in the Family History Collection of Terry Martin.)

One of Hart's grandsons, Henry Lea Hillman, was featured in this September 1969 issue of Forbes. One of Pittsburgh's leading philanthropists, Henry Lea died in 2017 at 98 years old. (Magazine cover web image.)

Thomas Tennessee Hillman (February 2, 1844—August 4, 1905) and wife Emily Gentry Hillman (March 19, 1844—1917). In comparison to his large and muscular older brother Hart, T.T. was a small man who dealt with health setbacks from childhood on. Yet he was bigger than life in the development of Birmingham, with investments in steel, coal, and railroads. He died in Atlantic City, his wife and two sisters, Nannie and Grace, at his side. His death was followed by a huge outpouring of grief by the citizens of Birmingham. With a $2 million fortune at his death, to each of his sisters he bequeathed $100,000. Emily, his wife, was the younger sister to Mary, her father-in-law Daniel's second wife. After T.T.'s death, and being childless, she financially assisted her husband's Hillman half-brothers, who were also her own nephews. Despite their role in the development of Birmingham, T.T. and Emily are buried at Mt. Olivet in Nashville near to Daniel and Mary, with accompanying extravagant monuments. The photo was made in Los Angeles, and indeed they had a California vacation home. (Vintage photo in the possession of Kenneth Thomson.)

This postcard, addressed to Nannie in 1904, depicts T.T. and Emily's home in Birmingham. The message from Emily indicates they are soon to leave for California. T.T. died the following year. (Postcard from the Family History Collection of Terry Martin.)

Grace Cora Hillman (July 16, 1858—November 4, 1936). She was Nannie's sister, though a bigger woman than the diminutive Nannie. She was the youngest of the four siblings born to Daniel Hillman by his first wife, Ann Jones Marable Hillman. In time she married David Campbell Scales, and they raised their family in Nashville. Engaging, energetic, and humorous, Grace involved herself in social and charitable causes. Grace Street, running by McFerrin Park, is named for her. The name "Grace", begun at least with her grandmother, Grace Huston Haines Hillman, has recurred with regularity among her descendants. (Vintage photo in the possession of Kenneth Thomson.)

Mary A. Gentry (August 5, 1841—May 18, 1908 are tombstone dates; the Gentry Family Bible indicates she was born August 15, 1840) was the first daughter of Meredith Poindexter Gentry, who served as both a U.S. and a Confederate Congressman, and of Emily Saunders Gentry, his first wife. Inscribed on the rear of the photo, "Miss Mary Gentry—1st daughter of M.P. Gentry in Mammoth Cave costume 1865." That was the year she married the widowed Daniel Hillman. She was only seven years older than her stepdaughter, Nannie. Mary and Daniel had four sons together. Outliving her husband by 23 years, she died at their Trigg Furnace home and is buried with him at Mt. Olivet Cemetery in Nashville. (Vintage photo in the Family History Collection of Terry Martin.)

Mary Gentry and Daniel Hillman's children (Nannie's half-brothers) are shown here (left to right): Meredith Poindexter Gentry Hillman (1868-1944), James Hoggatt Hillman (1870-1918), and Daniel C. Hillman (1867-1889). Not shown is a fourth boy who lived only a year, Bellfield Carter Hillman (1875-1876), and a eulogy of Mary indicates a daughter did not survive. Maturing during a time when their father Daniel's iron industry was not as prosperous as it had been, they did not benefit from his earlier wealth to the degree his first four children by Ann Marable did, and he was a mental wreck by the time of his death in 1885 before the boys had quite grown up. Son "Dan" would die at 22 of cancer, and though their older half-brother, T. T. Hillman, helped boost the careers of the other two, "Gentry" and "Jim" in Birmingham, they would struggle with sundry adversities. Gentry and wife Lallie Wooldridge had no children. Jim married Knoxie Polk Walker, and their troubled tale is related in the family memoir, <u>Sweet Mystery: A Book of Remembering</u>, by their granddaughter, author Judith Hillman Paterson. See 'For Further Reading' list. (Vintage photo in the possession of Thomas D. Martin.)

Daniel Hillman also fathered two children outside his two marriages. Knowing her to be his daughter (left), Mary Ann Hillman (1834-1873) was raised in the home at the insistence of Daniel's first wife, Ann Jones Marable Hillman. In time Mary married Dr. Caldwell "Kit" Barbour and had a family, though she and her husband both died young. Daniel left a legacy for their children in his will. Daniel also had a son (right) by way of an enslaved African-American. This son's name was John W. Hillman (1848-1911), who claimed Daniel as his father and whose descendants' relationship is proven by DNA evidence. John served for years as a hotel steward and then for many years as Custodian of the City Building of Covington, Kentucky. He was Grand Treasurer of his local Masonic Lodge chapter and was highly regarded in the community. He married Ellen Putney in 1870. (Vintage photo of Mary Ann Hillman Barbour in the Family History Collection of Terry Martin. Photo of John W. Hillman gleaned from <u>Biographical Sketches of Prominent Negro Men and Women of Kentucky</u>, published in 1897.)

Daniel Hillman and second wife Mary Gentry Hillman acquired this Nashville home in 1867. It is speculated by some to be the work of Adolphus Heiman, one of Nashville's premier architects of the 1850s. (The Hillmans also had a home nearer to the iron works operations in Kentucky.) Nannie and Edward's wedding was held here, and they lived here for much of the 1870s while Edward alternated between serving as a physician and as a clerk in the Hillman's iron store. The house was later demolished. Southern Methodist Publishing House (now the offices of Morgan and Morgan) replaced it in 1904. (Original photograph in the Family History Collection of Terry Martin.)

Ads appearing in the Nashville Union and American demonstrate the products sold by D. Hillman & Sons. Their Nashville store was located at 52 and 54 North Market Street. Edward worked here for his in-laws intermittently during the 1870s. By the time these ads were made, Daniel's brother, Charles Ellis Hillman, had sold out of his share of the business, as beforehand it had been known as Hillman, Bro. and Sons. (Web screenshots from the Nashville Union and American, June 25, 1874 and April 3, 1874.)

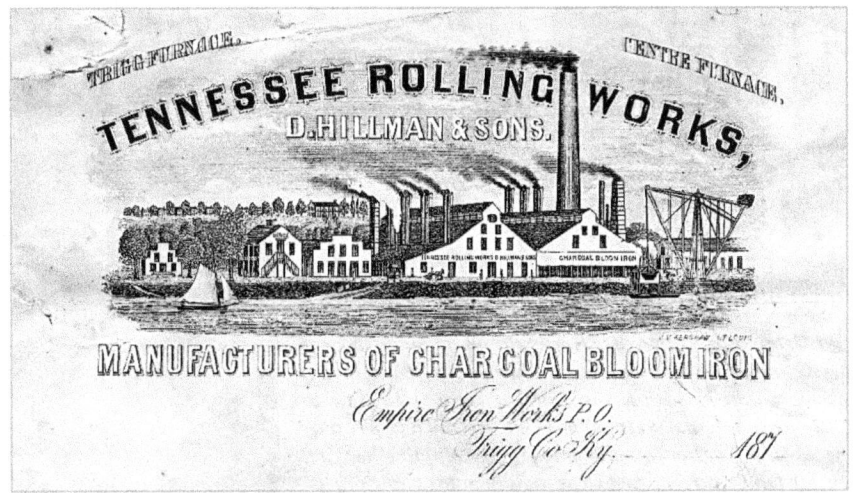

Letterhead featuring Daniel Hillman's operations in Kentucky. Though some sites were flooded with the creation of Lake Barkley in the 1960s, ruins of Center Furnace can still be seen in Land Between the Lakes National Recreation Area. (Original letterhead stationery in the Family History Collection of Terry Martin.)

Restored in 2016, the grave of James Franklin (1755-1828) resides in shadow. Patriarch of the Franklin clan, James arrived in Middle Tennessee in the 1770s after serving in Lord Dunmore's War and the Revolution. He defended Mansker's Station and other frontier sites from Indian attacks. With wife Mary, from the eminent Lauderdale family of Virginia, he sired ten children, in addition to a Franklin son from another woman. Close to the grave, their home "Pilot Knob" on Station Camp Creek was heavily damaged in its long history by two tornadoes, and though portions of it are original, with newer construction it resembles little the house of James and Mary. It is now referred to as "Golden Era Plantation." (Photo by Sandra Galbraith Long, Franklin descendant, at the D.A.R. grave restoration ceremony in Hendersonville, Tennessee in 2016.)

Isaac Franklin (May 26, 1789—April 27, 1846), son of James and Mary, was John Armfield's senior business partner in the slave trade and great uncle to Edward, author of the letters. Isaac had vast wealth with five plantations in Louisiana, Fairvue in Gallatin, 600 slaves in Louisiana, 150 in Tennessee, not to mention the fortune he acquired in the slave trade. Determined to settle into plantation life and remove some of the social stigma attached to the trade, he died within a few short years of retiring from the latter. Though older histories attempt to paint Franklin and Armfield as compassionate, making effort to keep slave families together, these wistful notions have been largely debunked by more recent research. (Washington B. Cooper portrait, 1845 same-artist copy of an earlier portrait. Image courtesy of Belmont Mansion.)

Adelicia Hayes Franklin (March 15, 1817—May 4, 1887) at Isaac's death might well have been the wealthiest widow in the country. She then married Col. Joseph Acklen and built Belmont in Nashville. Her children by Isaac did not survive childhood, though she has descendants from Joseph. Upon his death she married yet a third time to William Cheatham, but that marriage was not a happy one. She and some of her familial entourage, including her first two husbands, are buried in a monumental vault on the grounds of Mt. Olivet in Nashville. Her life story, a Scarlett O'Hara-like adventure, is retold at Belmont, open to the public. (Portrait miniature by John W. Dodge, 1857, after she married Acklen. Image courtesy of Belmont Mansion.)

"Fairvue." This 1994 painting by Cass Holly depicts the estate of Isaac Franklin and Adelicia Hayes Franklin in Gallatin. Still standing, recent modernizations have caused its National Historic Landmark status to be revoked, yet it is still impressive with its broad views of Old Hickory Lake. Some of its early buildings, overseer's house, and conical-roofed ice house (the latter shown in the left side of the image) can still be seen today. The artist, a Gallatin native, is a descendant of Judge Josephus Conn Guild, mentioned in one of Edward's letters. (Image courtesy of the artist).

Nephew to Isaac, Dr. John Washington Franklin (August 14, 1819—February 28, 1905) grew up with a large number of siblings in another plantation not far from Fairvue, where the Sumner County Convention and Visitor's Bureau now stands on Nashville Pike. He graduated from Transylvania Medical University in 1841 and married Florida Mercer Noel, daughter of the Rev. Silas Mercer Noel, a prominent Baptist minister from Frankfort. Edward, author of the letters, was the last of their three children, the others being John Armfield Franklin and Adele. Florida died two years after Edward was born, and John Washington turned his children over to his sister Martha and her husband John Armfield to raise. He then married Sarah Baber, built the home "Oakley," and had nine more children, though he retained strong ties with his three by Florida, influencing Edward's choice of a medical career. John Washington served as a physician in the Confederate Army. The two images show John Washington in different eras of his life. He is buried at the Gallatin City Cemetery. No known images exist of Edward's mother, Florida. (Vintage images in the possession of Kenneth Thomson, the first a daguerreotype.)

"Maywood" was where Edward Noel Franklin was born to his parents, Dr. John Washington Franklin and Florida Mercer Noel Franklin in 1846. Built in 1838, the home in downtown Gallatin, sometimes referred to as the "Trousdale-Baskerville House," was added to the National Register of Historic Places in 2009 after being restored. For a brief time the family moved to New Orleans where Florida died of "ship fever" (typhus) in January 1848, and John Washington returned her body to be buried in her hometown of Frankfort, Kentucky. (Editor's Image.)

"Oakley" on Nashville Pike in Gallatin was constructed in the Gothic Revival style in 1852. Both William Strickland and Adolphus Heiman, two eminent architects of Nashville, have been speculated to be responsible for its design. It was built by John Washington Franklin for his second wife, Sarah Baber, on property she inherited. Here they raised nine children. They also bred horses, a common business operation among the Franklin kin of those earlier generations. (Image by Lyn Franklin Hoyt, a descendant of John and Sarah.)

John Armfield (1797—September 20, 1871). Business partner to Isaac Franklin in the slave-trading firm, Franklin and Armfield, John married Isaac's niece, Martha Franklin, in 1834. With his fortune from the slave trade, John Armfield enhanced the resort at Beersheba Springs, Tennessee, reopening it on the eve of the Civil War. He was also an early patron of the University of the South at Sewanee. As a slave trader he has, like Isaac, become a notorious figure in American history, yet he was dear to the three Franklin children, for whom he acted as a father figure. Edward, author of the letters, was at his bedside when he died. John is buried in the Armfield Cemetery in Beersheba Springs. (Image courtesy of the Tennessee State Library and Archives. See discussion of this image under "Armfield Family" in "Sources.")

Martha Franklin Armfield (1815—1904) was the daughter of Isaac Franklin's brother, John Franklin, and his wife, Elizabeth Rawlings Franklin. As sister to Dr. John Washington Franklin, she was Edward's aunt, and raised Edward and his siblings after their mother died. She also raised their older cousin, Blanche Franklin, another niece by way of a different brother. After John Armfield died, Martha lived in Maryland for a time with her nieces' families, and in the last years of her life she returned home to Sumner County, remaining in the care of other relatives. She died with little to her name, despite her husband's once large fortune. She is buried at the Gallatin City Cemetery. (Editor's 2017 snapshot from framed image at the Armfield home in Beersheba Springs.)

"Hard Times" was built in the 1820s during a depression, and this was its name when the Armfields bought it and moved in with the Franklin children in 1849. They lived here until 1855. Now known in Hendersonville, Tennessee as "Spring Haven Mansion," close to Blue Grass Country Club, it is now a private event facility, the site of numerous weddings and receptions. A descriptive historical marker near the entrance highlights its history and the Armfield era. (Editor's image.)

The three grown children of Dr. John Washington Franklin and his first wife, Florida Mercer Noel Franklin. They were raised by their aunt and uncle, Martha and John Armfield. From left to right: John Armfield Franklin (named obviously for John Armfield, a friend of John Washington Franklin's), Dr. Edward Noel Franklin, author of the letters, and Adele Franklin. (Original image in the Family History Collection of Terry Martin.)

Edward Noel Franklin (October 20, 1846—November 21, 1909) stands in the center. This first image, taken at a studio in Philadelphia, likely shows him with medical school classmates at the University of Pennsylvania where he graduated in 1869. Afterwards, he worked in a hospital in Galveston, Texas, but upon hearing of his Uncle Armfield's downturn in health, he dutifully returned to nurse the man who had been as a father to him. The second image (below) shows him possibly around the time he met Nannie in 1871. (Both original images in the possession of Thomas D. Martin.)

John Armfield Franklin (January 25, 1843—November 16, 1871), the "idolized brother" of Edward. John in the first image (right) is in his cadet uniform, likely at the Kentucky Military Institute. He later served in C.S.A. 7th Tennessee Infantry, and 13th Virginia Cavalry, altogether four years, surrendering his arms at Appomattox. Passionate diary fragments exist of his last months in the war. The second image (left —sometimes mistakenly attributed to John Armfield rather than John Armfield Franklin) is of an original crystoleum. The

third image (below left) shows him in the late 1860s with moustache and longer hair reminiscent of his brother. After the war, John was employed as a drummer in the whiskey business in Louisville, where he fell in with a woman by the name of Alice. Edward refers to her once in the letters as his brother's "wife," but it eventually became known she was his paramour, a "beautiful siren" who "wound her toils about him," according to the newspaper. Yet it is as easy to imagine the young buck taking advantage of money, privilege, and distance from home in order to get what he wanted, and he certainly had male antecedents who had dallied outside the confines of marriage. Alice was with him when he died—within two months of his eponymous uncle—in Tallahassee, Florida, of pneumonia. A devastated Edward met his brother's body by train and took possession of his personal effects in Washington, Georgia, and he was buried in Sumner County. (First two original images and photocopied newspaper notice in the possession of Kenneth Thomson. Third original photo in the possession of Thomas D. Martin.)

FUNERAL NOTICE.

DIED at Tallahassee, Florida, November 16, 1871, JNO. ARMFIELD, eldest son of Dr. Jno. W Franklin.

The funeral will take place tomorrow (Thursday) morning at 10 o'clock. Funeral Sermon, at the residence of the family, by Rev. Mr. Boude.

GALLATIN, Nov. 22, 1871.

Adele Franklin (November 29, 1845—December 5, 1921), Edward's sister. In the first photo (right), Adele appears at 13 years old. Highly educated, Adele attended Nashville Female Academy and Patapsco Institute near Baltimore. The image (below right) is upon her marriage to George L. Van Bibber in Beersheba Springs on August 3, 1871 at the very time Edward began writing his letters to Nannie. He expresses great affection for his sister who moved away with her new husband to Bel Air, Maryland. Adele has many descendants. The image (below left) was given by Adele to Nannie marked "For dear Nannie with my best love," and it is possible it was by way of their friendship that Edward met his future wife. At bottom is the newspaper quote describing Adele's wedding at Beersheba Springs. (First two images in the possession of Kenneth Thomson, the first an original ambrotype. The third original image in the possession of Thomas D. Martin.)

A brilliant wedding was celebrated at Beersheba last week. Miss Adele Franklin, daughter of our respected and well known fellow-citizen, Dr. John Franklin, was married at the residence of her uncle, Col. Jno. Armfield, to Geo. L. Van Bibber, a talented and promising young member of the Baltimore bar. It was a most magnificent affair, rivalling the good old times that distinguished our country before the war. Mrs. Armfield surpassed herself in getting up the wedding supper, and was truly elegant, eliciting the praise of all who were present on the happy occasion.

--<u>The Examiner</u>, Gallatin, Tenn., Saturday, August 19, 1871

Capt. Alexander James Porter (1822-1888) from Nashville was one of Edward's friends mentioned often in his letters. His first wife, Martha Watson, was a distant cousin of Nannie's but died shortly after he sold the Porter family home, Tammany Wood (now Riverwood Mansion), to the Cooper family in 1859. Tragically, their son Jimmy drowned in the Cumberland River in 1866. Though their daughter married, there were no children. However, his second wife, Rebecca Greer Allison, the "Mrs. Porter" in Edward's letters, does have descendants, including from the son born to her in Beersheba in September of 1871. (Oil on canvas, app. 1840. Artist unknown. Image from the Tennessee Portrait Project website.)

Capt. William G. Ewin (1842-1882). Martha Jane "Mattie" Hillman Ewin (1848-1926). The Ewins are mentioned often in Edward's letters after he moved to Nashville. William's leg was amputated in the war, but this did not end a disciplined work ethic. At the time Edward was writing the letters, Capt. Ewin was Davidson County Court Clerk. Mattie was William's second wife and Nannie's first cousin, being the daughter of George W. Hillman, Daniel Hillman's brother. As indicated in the letters, she was seriously ill that fall of 1871. They had several children, and she survived him, so she clearly recovered from her illness. Eventually moving to Waverly, Tennessee, Mattie helped establish the Waverly Church of Christ. (Left image in the possession of Thomas D. Martin. Right image in the Family History Collection of Terry Martin.)

Matilda Franklin (1828—February 10, 1878) is mentioned as one of the servants who was to travel with Aunt Martha to Baltimore after the death of John Armfield. A slave belonging initially to John Franklin, Martha's father, who owned a plantation with 99 slaves where the Sumner County Convention and Visitor's Bureau now stands on Nashville Pike, she remained with Martha until the end of Matilda's life at 50. The building housing the Bureau is not the original John Franklin plantation home, which was torn down in the early half of the twentieth century. If as indicated in the obituary Matilda was buried in the graveyard of her former mistress, this would be in reference to Elizabeth Rawlings (Mrs. John) Franklin, the mother of Martha and of John Washington Franklin. This grave plot is located in Stoneridge Farms apartment complex, across from the Bureau. It is believed some slaves are buried in the fenced-in plot with the family, though not all graves are marked. (Image above, courtesy of the Tennessee State Library and Archives. Image has been altered from the original: the boundary was cropped. Obituary from <u>The Daily American</u>, Nashville, March 3, 1878. Copy provided by Kenneth Thomson.)

Died, in Sumner county, Feb. 10, 1878, MATILDA FRANKLIN, colored, aged 50 years, the life-long, faithful and affectionate servant of Mrs. Martha Armfield.

She was a consistent member of the Episcopal church, and a regular communicant of Christ Church, Nashville, and had the respect of all who knew her. She took great interest in all the charities of the church, (being an active member of the Parish Aid Society), working cheerfully for the ladies' societies and accounting promptly for all money collected for them.

It was her pleasure to wait on and minister to the sick and the distressed. She was thoroughly honest and truthful, and was noted for her modest and correct deportment.

The kind nursing and tender care bestowed on her during her last illness in the home of her former owners was a touching and deserved tribute to her worth. She was aware of her approaching death, but said she felt no fears, saw her way clear and expected to meet her friends in heaven. One of her last requests was to be buried in her old mistresses' graveyard, which was complied with, and her remains were followed to the grave by all the members of the family she had known and loved all her life.

Although retiring and diffident, she never missed an opportunity to speak a kind word of advice and counsel to both white and colored friends, often assuring the latter that to be respected and have friends they must do right and respect themselves.

She did her part well, and although in an humble station, her exemplary life and triumphant death are a bright example for us all.   A.

Dr. Edward Noel Franklin. This photo was taken at the time of his marriage to Nannie Hillman, which took place on January 3, 1872. (Original photo in the Family History Collection of Terry Martin.)

Mrs. Edward Noel Franklin (Nannie Hillman Franklin) on January 3, 1872. (Original photo in the Family History Collection of Terry Martin.)

Order from.
                Mrs. Daniel Hillman
to be ready by January 3rd
                1872.

1 Large Lady Cake with Raisins.
        Basket in Center
Gold Leaves, Hexigon Shape, about 15.00

1 Large Dark Fruit Cake
        Thick though.
    Round Mould   about 25.00

1 Large Lady Cake with Citron
        Basket in Center
Silver Leaves, Hexigon Shape about 15.00

1 Lady Cake Large Sure White.
Handsomely Ornamented
    Thick & Round Mould about 18.00

1 Large White Mountain
    Cake. Square. —

Page 1 of a 3-page bill for food and confections for Edward and Nannie's wedding banquet. See the Afterword for detail. (Original order in the Family History Collection of Terry Martin.)

Edward and Nannie attended a reception in Nashville for President and Mrs. Rutherford B. Hayes in 1877. (Original invitation in the Family History Collection of Terry Martin.)

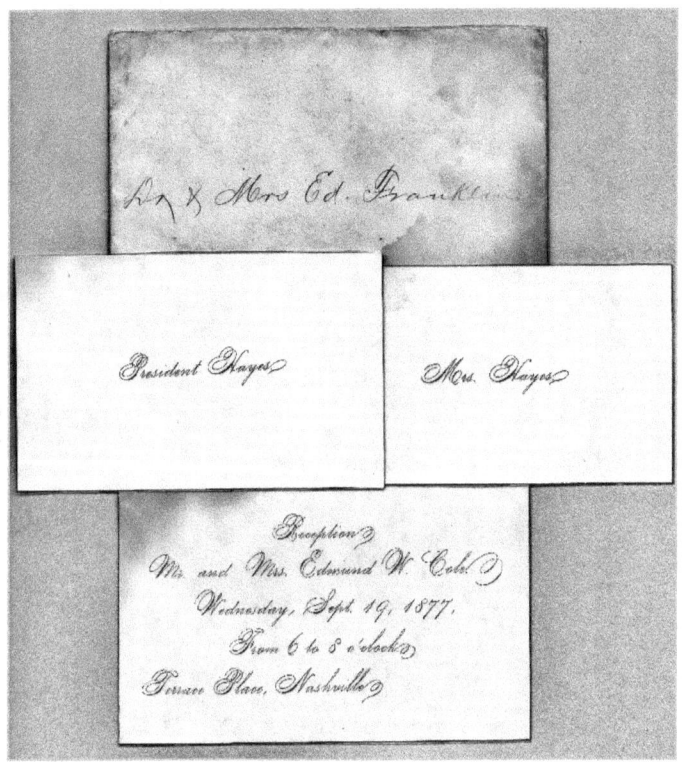

"Lone Pine" was the North Water Street residence of Edward and Nannie in Gallatin after their first years in Nashville and Mitchellville. Four generations spent various eras of their lives here. Daughter Grace lived here all her life raising her daughter Allen Palmer. Allen Palmer's wedding took place here, and her children were born in and lived in the home for many years. Sold in the 1950s, it was subsequently torn down to make room for Gallatin Nursing Home. (Original photo in the Family History Collection of Terry Martin.)

Edward and Nannie's first four children. Oldest to youngest, Florida, Grace, Daniel Hillman, and Edward Noel, Jr. Two others, Nannie Marable, and Charles Hillman were born later. Edward Noel, Jr., (this is the only known photo showing him—the smallest child) and Nannie Marable did not survive childhood. (Vintage photo, app. 1880, in the Family History Collection of Terry Martin.)

Florida Franklin (October 29, 1872—June 17, 1965), oldest child of Edward and Nannie. She received her education at Howard Female College in Gallatin and Columbia Institute in Maury County, Tennessee. In time she married Walter L. Anderson of Gallatin, an insurance salesman. Florida is still fondly remembered today by older Gallatin residents. (Original images in the possession of Kenneth Thomson.)

Grace Franklin (October 22, 1874—June 22, 1942), the second child of Edward and Nannie. Like Florida she also received her education from Howard Female College and Columbia Institute. She later married Allen Luke Palmer House of a prominent Gallatin family. He died shortly afterwards, leaving her pregnant with their only child, and Grace remained a widow for life. The two images show Grace as a young girl and then as a young widow. Founding regent of the local D.A.R. chapter, she was also a fine artist. (Vintage photos in the Family History Collection of Terry Martin.)

Daniel Hillman Franklin (September 24, 1876—October 13, 1904), called "Hillman." Three letters exist in the editor's collection written by Hillman to his mother from Webb boarding school in Bell Buckle, Tennessee. Later an employee of the L & N Railroad, and popular in Gallatin, Hillman died tragically of morphine poisoning following attempts to overcome a drug habit. The first image shows him as a boy and the second as a young man, possibly within a few years of his premature death. He is buried at Mt. Olivet in Nashville. (Vintage photos in the possession of Kenneth Thomson.)

Nannie Marable Franklin (January 20, 1884—November 24, 1885). Baby portrait, baptismal record, and a lock of red hair remain to document the brief life of "Little Nannie." She died at 22 months. One brother, Edward Noel Franklin, Jr., (October 21, 1879 — November 14, 1884) lived only five years. He appears as the smallest child in the group photo on page 104. Both are buried at Mt. Olivet. (Photographic image in the possession of Kenneth Thomson. Baptismal record and lock of hair in the Family History Collection of Terry Martin.)

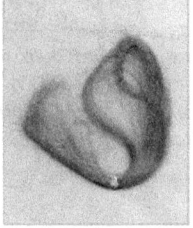

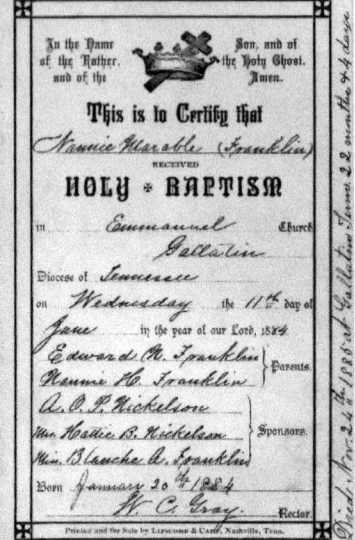

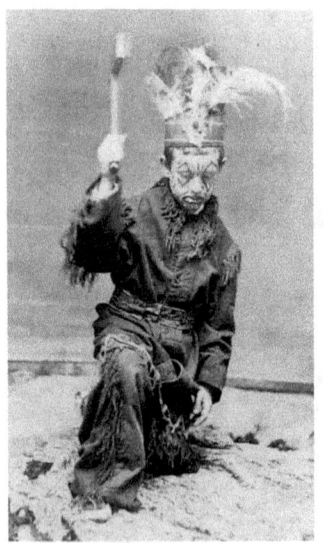

Charles Hillman Franklin (September 19, 1886-November 23, 1954) was the sixth and last child of Edward and Nannie. These images show Charlie as a boy and later in uniform in World War I. After his first marriage ended in divorce, he met a young French woman during the war, Alexandrine Groslevin, called "Didine." Their marriage was life-long. (First image, original in the possession of Kenneth Thomson. Second original image in the possession of Genie Borcher Riddle.)

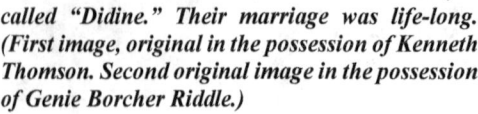

Drug Habit Cured at Home by Dr. Ed N. Franklin, Gallatin, Tenn.

After years of investigation, we discovered a rational treatment for the "drug habit," and now offer to the public a treatment that meets every requirement. We cure the patient without nervous shock or any pain. They are more comfortable after taking the first dose of medicine than while taking the drug, and will continue to feel better from day to day. There is no weakness or debility by the treatment. The patient feels that he is cured from the very beginning of the treatment.

Dr. Edward Noel Franklin. These images show a somewhat older Edward than the one taken the day he married Nannie. (The middle initial "M" in the photo caption below is an error.) It was his oldest granddaughter, Allen Palmer House, who marked the cut-out "Grandfather" in her handwriting. The above ad, taken from the May 1903 edition of Confederate Veteran, advertises Edward's supposed new drug addiction cure. Ironically, his oldest son, Hillman, succumbed to his own drug habit. (First image, original photo in the possession of Kenneth Thomson. Newspaper cut-out in the Family History Collection of Terry Martin. The drug cure ad is a web screenshot from Confederate Veteran magazine.)

R. M. RICHARDSON,   DR. ED. M. FRANKLIN,
T. W. LELLYETT,   JOHN E. TURNEY,

Grandfather

Officers of the Hagey Institute of Nashville.
[See page 18.]

Standing on the far right is an older Nannie next to her oldest brother, John Hartwell "Hart" Hillman. The couple on the left are their younger sister, Grace Cora, and her husband, David Campbell Scales. A photo likely taken within a year or two of the death in 1905 of their brother T. T. Hillman, the palm trees suggest it was at his San Diego vacation home where they would visit.

This portrait (left) is of a mature Nannie. (Both original images in the Family History Collection of Terry Martin.)

A three-generation portrait (bottom left) shows Nannie with daughter Grace Franklin House, and Grace's daughter, Allen Palmer House. The little girl was named for her father, Allen Luke Palmer House (bottom right), who died of typhoid just months before her birth. Born in 1898, she was the first grandchild of Edward and Nannie, and spent most of her life in Gallatin. In time she married Oscar Eugene Martin, a civil engineer from North Carolina. They have many descendants, some still in Gallatin. Oscar and Allen Palmer were instrumental in the restoration of Historic Rugby, Tennessee, where they kept a summer home. Allen Palmer died in 1993. (Left original image in the Family History Collection of Terry Martin. Right original image in the possession of Noel P. Martin.)

A 1909 portrait (right) shows the family of Edward and Nannie's oldest daughter, Florida Franklin Anderson. Her husband, Walter Leake Anderson, was an insurance salesman. Sara McFerrin Anderson, the girl on the far left, was born in 1906 and grew up in Gallatin, eventually marrying Walton Maxey Jarman, a founder of Genesco, Inc. They raised their family in Nashville, and there are many Jarman descendants today. Sara Mac died in 1997. Sara Mac's younger sister, Grace Adele Anderson, born in 1908, lived nearly all her life in Gallatin and never married. She was greatly loved by everyone in town who knew her, a fun cousin and aunt to Allen Palmer's and Sara Mac's children and grandchildren. Grace Adele died in 2003. (Original image in the Family History Collection of Terry Martin.)

In one of the last known photographs featuring Nannie (left), son Charlie in uniform stands behind, looking upon his first daughter, little Florida. Charlie's French wife, Didine, is in the left of the picture, and the child's Aunt Grace is in the patterned dress. To date the photo, little Florida was born in 1921. Florida in time married Charles Allen Borcher, Jr., and they have many descendants. Florida died in 2017. (Original image in the possession of Genie Borcher Riddle.)

This shows Charlie once more and his two daughters, Florida and baby Nan (born in 1927), the latter in her Aunt Grace's lap. Charlie's family lived in Washington in order for him to pursue an army career, where he achieved the rank of colonel. Nan in time married John Beeman Kirkpatrick II. They have many descendants. Nan died in 2015. The photo was taken five years after grandmother Nannie died, who thus never met her namesake and last grandchild. (Original image in the Family History Collection of Terry Martin.)

Beersheba Springs, Tennessee. The big hotel is only part of a complex, some of it enhanced and some of it newly built by John Armfield before the Civil War. Following the war and the reopening, Armfield remained in Beersheba until his death in 1871. Wife Martha then went to her nieces in Maryland, and Edward moved to establish his medical practice in Nashville. Aunt Martha was not buried with her husband on the mountain, but rather returned in time to Sumner County in the care of relatives. She is buried in Gallatin. The resort experienced good times in subsequent years, but the Depression hit in the 1930s, and it was sold to the Methodist Church, which uses it today for retreats. In this 2017 image, the editor's sons stand on the steps as an antique car pulls up. (Editor's image.)

At the Armfield's old house in Beersheba Springs, U.S. and Tennessee flags announce the presence of modern-day vacationers. To this home on the Cumberland Plateau, John and Martha Armfield moved in the late 1850s with Edward and the other two Franklin children from Sumner County. Armfield poured his wealth into the purchase of the home and resort, remodeling, constructing additions and new buildings, and reopening it to acclaim on the eve of war. Edward wrote most of his letters to Nannie from here in 1871. (Editor's image.)

Still used today are a red and white linen tablecloth with twelve matching napkins once belonging to Nannie. On that tablecloth is shown here the traveling lap desk acquired by Edward in 1870, and upon which he wrote some of his letters to Nannie that following year. (Tablecloth and lap desk in the possession of Terry Martin. Editor's images.)

A sample of Edward's writing on one of the twenty-seven original letters and the only envelope that was saved along with them. (Original letters and envelope in the Family History Collection of Terry Martin. Editor's images.)

The editor, Terry Martin, stands next to the massive Daniel and Mary Gentry Hillman monument at Mt. Olivet Cemetery in Nashville. Just a few feet away stands that of Daniel's son T.T. and his wife Emily. Sara Franklin Homer of New Jersey took these photos during a family treasure hunt with the editor in the spring of 2014, her brother Ernest Franklin of Nashville also present. Interestingly, Sara and Ernest are not only Franklin descendants by way of John Washington Franklin's second wife, Sarah Baber, they also come from the Hillman family by way of a second Franklin-Hillman connection. Their mother was a descendant of Grace Cora Hillman Scales, Nannie's sister. Sadly, Sara succumbed to her battle with cancer only a few months after this cemetery outing, but her love of exploring family history is shared by many who knew her.

Not far from the Hillman monuments are the gravestones of Edward and Nannie. Four of their six children are buried next to them: Grace, Hillman, Edward, Jr., and little Nannie. Florida is buried at the Gallatin City Cemetery, and Charlie is buried at Arlington National Cemetery. (Editor's images.)

At the 1884 home, Kingstone Lisle, in Rugby, Tennessee, a log-cabin-patterned quilt made by Nannie graces the bed. Both Nannie's mother, Ann Jones Marable Hillman, and daughter, Grace Franklin House, were quilt makers as well. Appropriate to the era, this quilt was donated to Historic Rugby by Nannie's granddaughter, Allen Palmer House Martin. The Martins were instrumental in restoring this British-American village, set rather like Beersheba Springs on the lovely Cumberland Plateau. Kingstone Lisle and other key buildings are open to the public for tours. (Editor's image.)

The editor, Terry Martin, with his sons, Luke and Drew in 2012. The boys sit in the carriage once belonging to Edward and Nannie, their great-great-great-grandparents. The restored carriage is on display at Wynnewood State Historic Site in Castalian Springs, Tennessee. (Snapshot image by Laura Sund Martin.)

Appendix 1

Selected Newspaper Articles Relevant to, and the Final Tennessee State Supreme Court Report of,

Franklin v. Franklin

"One of the most celebrated law suits that was ever in the courts at Gallatin"

--<u>The Daily American</u>
Nashville, Tenn., Friday, February 27, 1891

A very brief analysis of this court case between Edward and his father, Dr. John Washington Franklin, over the late-found will of Edward's brother, John Armfield Franklin, is described in my Afterword on pages 75-76. I am grateful to Michael Ponce of Ponce Law of Nashville for reading the final Supreme Court report, reviewing my summary from the Afterword, and ensuring that I had interpreted the final verdict correctly (though roughly, as there are details that were unnecessary as part of the Afterword). According to Kenneth Thomson, President of the Sumner County Historical Society, there are voluminous records on this case at the Sumner County Archives. These articles and the Supreme Court report transcribed here are meant to provide the reader additional insight on the details and to get a better sense for the notoriety of the case at the time it was taking place.

The Examiner
Gallatin, Tenn. (Year 1887, uncertain date)
Holographic Will Case.
Franklin vs. Franklin Occupies the Week--Sensational Evidence.

    Almost the entire week of the circuit court, Judge Munford presiding, has been occupied with the trial of a holographic will case involving quite a large amount of property, accompanied with evidence quite sensational and out of the usual run in will cases. To render the case still more remarkable it is a contest in which the parties bear the relation of father and son, being Dr. John W. Franklin, a prominent citizen and well known physician of repute, and Dr. Ed N. Franklin, also a physician of excellent standing. The latter married Miss Hillman, the daughter of the wealthy iron man of Nashville.
    It would require many columns of the Examiner to give in full the vast amount of oral and written testimony in the case, but we will endeavor to condense it so that the leading facts may be understood.
    Dr. John W. Franklin has been twice married, his first wife being Miss Florida Noel of Lexington, Ky., a daughter of Rev. Silas M. Noel, (Ed. note. the Noel family was from Frankfort, though Lexington was the last church assignment for Silas before he died. All the Noels, including Florida, are buried at Frankfort

Cemetery.) a distinguished Baptist minister in his day, and the founder Georgetown, Ky., male college. She will be remembered by our older citizens as a most lovely and charming lady. Three children were born to them—John Armfield, Edward N. and Adele. The daughter was married to a Mr. Van Bibber of Belle Air, Md., a gentleman of wealth, and is living there at present. The elder son, Armfield, never married. The mother died very young many years before the war. The second wife of Dr. John W. was a Miss Baber, a daughter of the late Thomas A. Baber, and sister of John T. Baber. A large family of children have been the fruit of the second marriage.

And now we arrive at the period which gives rise to the will suit.

Sometime after the close of the war, the elder son, Armfield, was employed as a drummer by a wholesale whisky house of Louisville, and traveled in the South. During his stay in Louisville he unfortunately fell into the company of a "strange woman," who wound her toils about him. It was not in proof that he was generally dissolute, but in a weak moment he fell a victim to the beautiful siren. In the fall of 1871 she accompanied him, upon a tour to Georgia and Florida. She was represented as being married to him, which was done out of regard to the proprieties of life. During the journey he was taken sick at Tallahassee, Fla., and died in a short time. His effects consisted only of a traveling trunk and a gun box, containing an English fowling piece, with its accoutrements. We will note here that the gun had been presented to him by his uncle, John Armfield, who was a millionaire and partner of the late Isaac Franklin, the owner of Fairview, and of great plantations and thousands of slaves in Louisiana. This box figures prominently in the will case now on trial.

The intelligence of the death of Armfield Franklin was telegraphed to his brother, Dr. Ed N. Franklin, at Gallatin, by the attending physician, who was instructed in reply to ship the remains to Washington, Ga., where he would meet them, which was done and the body brought home and interred.

This was in November, 1871, nearly sixteen years ago. The trunk and gun box were brought along with the remains. The testimony is conflicting as to the whereabouts of the gun box up to 1885, being at Gallatin, Nashville, and Mitchellville, but it was most of the time in the possession of Dr. E. N. Franklin. He resided several years ago at Mitchellville, north of Gallatin, on the L. & N. and a few years ago removed to Gallatin to practice his profession. His office was at the drug store of Montgomery & Knight on the square. The gun had been unused all this time and he determined to clean it up at the drug store. The contents were taken out, and he placed the box bottom up to knock out the dust, when a paper fell out that had remained concealed under a plate in the corner. He examined it and at once saw that it purported to be a will, signed by his brother Armfield. It devised his one-fifth interest in the estate of his uncle John Armfield to him. It further directed him to pay "Alice" $500 and to provide her with a ticket from Florida to Louisville, her home. She is not spoken of as his wife. It is claimed and is evidence that he immediately exhibited the will to John W. Knight, the present druggist. Now it is denied by the other side that the will is in the handwriting of Armfield and charges are made that it has been forged. A large number of witnesses claiming to know the handwriting of the dead man affirm its genuineness. His associates in the army affirm that is his writing. It is not our province to discuss that as this is a matter for the jury to determine. Against the validity of the will it is urged by the lawyers that it was not found in a place where valuable papers are usually deposited and that the statutes and decisions sustain them on this point. On the other side it is urged that the testator acted with the greatest foresight and discretion; that if he had placed the will in his trunk it would have fallen at once into the hands of "Alice," who, discovering that she was cut out would destroy it, but would not be apt to examine the gun case.

All of these points were exhaustively argued by the attorneys on each side. For the will were R. K. Gillespie, T. C. Mulligan and Charles R. Head.
Against the will: S. F. Wilson and James J. Turner.
The amount involved in the case is quite large, say from $15,000 to $20,000.

In overlooking our rapid statement of the singular case we find that we have omitted to state that Dr. Jno. W. Franklin, *pere*, is the executor of the will of his brother-in-law John Armfield, in whose hands came the one-fifth interest of his son Armfield Franklin, now the object of contest in the court and which is claimed by Dr. Ed. N. Franklin under the holograph will in Florida.

The Examiner regrets the necessity of a report of family disagreements even when they get into courts for adjudication, and which is increased by our knowledge of the high standing of the parties and their relation in blood. But it is one of those 'causes celebre' which make their records and cannot be omitted by the faithful journalist. It naturally grows out of the distribution of accumulated wealth which originated out of the old regime of slave days when cotton was king in the south and the heirs have inherited its consequences. And even now other courts are in the process of deciding rights of the heirs of the old Franklin Louisiana and Sumner county property and the will of the mistress of Fairview is now in the hands of the lawyers at Nashville. The grandchildren of the old planter, Isaac Franklin, whose slaves in great gangs often passed through Gallatin on their way to the cotton fields of Louisiana, may be in their graves before all of their rights are determined. Fairview still stands in our midst. Its owners have all crossed the river. Its glories as a famous country farm, when the young folks danced and frolicked and made love, have passed away, and they even are now grandfathers and grandmothers or have been laid away to their final rest; its broad acres are green with blue grass where sport blooded horses under the eye of the turfman Charles Reed, and costly stables dot its ground where racing men congregate. Such is life.

The Examiner
Gallatin, Tenn. (Year 1887, uncertain date)
After a Third Trial a Verdict is Given in Favor of Dr. Ed. N. Franklin.

The celebrated will suit of Franklin vs. Franklin, involving some $15,000 to $20,000 worth of property, was decided Tuesday last, the jury holding that the will was valid. The nature of the suit is that Armfield Franklin died, leaving a will by which Ed. N. Franklin, his brother, was benefited. The will in dispute was found, as claimed by the beneficiary, in a gun-box left by the deceased at the time of his death in Florida ten years ago. Dr. Jno. W. Franklin, father of Armfield and Ed. N., was executor of the estate, and Ed. N. sued him for the money. It was claimed by the opposing party that the will is a forgery. The verdict of the jury sustains the will as to the personal property, which is the only property involved, there being no real estate.

The counsel in the case were C. R. Head, Jas. W. Blackmore, T. C. Mulligan and R. K. Gillespie for Dr. Ed. N. Franklin, and J. J. Turner, S. F. Wilson and B. D. Bell for Dr. Jno. W. Franklin.

The Examiner has more than once given its readers a full history of this remarkable case and will not now enter upon its details. If appealed to the supreme court it will become a cause celebre, and be recorded in the reports of that court.

The Daily American
Nashville, Tenn., Thursday, November 10, 1887
Page 7
Gallatin.
Special Dispatch to The American
The Franklin Will Case Decided at Gallatin
Gallatin, Tenn., Nov. 9.

—A decision was rendered to-day in the Circuit Court in the celebrated Franklin will case, the jury rendering a verdict settling up the will in dispute. In some respects it is one of the most interesting lawsuits ever tried in Sumner County. The parties to the suit are among the oldest and most reputable families, and, besides dollars and cents, involved the good name of the plaintiff in the case, who was, by inference at least, charged with forgery. Like all family lawsuits, the feeling on both sides was bitter, and the respective friends of both parties were more or less stirred up over the facts as developed on the trial. The parties to the suit bore the relation of father and son, being Dr. John W. Franklin, a prominent citizen and well-known physician of repute, and Dr. Ed. N. Franklin, also a physician of excellent standing. The latter married Miss Hillman, a daughter of the wealthy iron man of Nashville.

Dr. John W. Franklin, the defendant in the case, has been twice married— first to Miss Florence (ed. note: should be "Florida") Noel, of Kentucky, who bore him three children, Adele, Armfield and Ed N., the latter the plaintiff in the case. His second wife was Miss Baber, of this county. Sometime after the close of the war Armfield, the elder son, was employed as a drummer by a wholesale whisky house in Louisville, Ky., and traveled in the South. Here he became involved in affair of gallantry with a woman who accompanied him on his travels as his wife. In the fall of 1871 she went with him on a tour through Georgia and Florida. During the journey he was taken sick at Tallahassee, Fla., and died in a short time. His effects consisted only of a traveling trunk and a gun box, containing an English fowling piece with its accoutrements. His remains and effects were brought to Gallatin and interred (Ed. note. The precise location of John Armfield Franklin's burial is uncertain). This gun box figured prominently in the trial. The gun and box have remained since the death of the owner, Armfield Franklin, in the possession of his brother, Dr. Ed N. Franklin. In 1885, while giving the box and gun a cleaning out in the drug store of Montgomery

& Knight, in Gallatin, a paper fell out that had remained concealed under a plate in the corner of the box. He examined it and at once saw it purported to be a will, signed by his brother Armfield. It devised his one-fifth interest in the estate of his uncle, John Armfield, to him. It further directed him to pay "Alice," the woman with whom he had been living, $500 and to provide her with a ticket from Florida to Louisville, her home.

Dr. John W. Franklin, the administrator of the estate of John Armfield, denied the validity of the will and refused to pay over to Dr. Ed N. Franklin the share of his brother, Armfield, in the John Armfield estate, and for which Dr. Ed N. Franklin sues. The charge of forgery was argued by the defendant.

The case was tried before Judge Mumford last June, but the jury failed to agree upon a verdict. Another trial was had at this term of the court and a verdict rendered in favor of the plaintiff, thus declaring the will to be a genuine one. The amount involved is about $15,000. The lawyers in the case were C. R. Head, Jas. W. Blackmore, T. C. Mulligan and R. K. Gillespie for the plaintiff, and J. J. Turner and S. F. Wilson for the defendant. The case will probably be appealed.

The Daily American
Nashville, Tenn., Friday, March 7, 1890
Page 1
Franklin vs. Franklin: A Celebrated Case on Trial at Gallatin.
Gallatin, March 6. — (Special)

The celebrated will suit between Dr. John W. Franklin and Dr. Ed N. Franklin, who bear the relation of father and son, was begun here yesterday. The suit has been tried three times, and the facts have before been published in the American. The amount involved foots up many thousands of dollars. The will over which the suit was brought was that of Armfield Franklin, a brother of Dr. Ed. and son of Dr. John W., and was found in a gun box in the possession of Dr. Ed N. Franklin. Armfield was a drummer, and died at Tallahassee, Fla., in 1871, leaving his effects to Ed. N. Franklin; but the slip of paper purporting to be the will was not found until 1885. The first trial was a mistrial, the second a mistrial also, but nine of the jurymen were in favor of settling up the will. The third trial gave a verdict for Dr. Ed N. Franklin against his father. The case was taken to the Supreme Court, which in turn sent it back for a new trial. Suits have been going on ever since the supposed will was found. Some of the testimony is very entertaining.

The Daily American
Nashville, Tenn., Friday, March 14, 1890
Page 6
Celebrated Case: The Court Decides in Setting Up the Will of Armfield Franklin
Gallatin, March 13. — (Special.)

—For the third time the celebrated Franklin will case has been decided in favor of setting up the will of Armfield Franklin. This is a suit of son against father. Dr. Ed. N. Franklin brought suit against his father, Dr. John W. Franklin, for the recovery of property left him by his brother, Armfield Franklin. This is the exact will, and was reported to have been found in the gun-box given to Dr. Ed. N. Franklin. The will reads:

Washington, Ga., Oct., 1871.—This is my last will and testament. I will and bequeath to my brother, Edward N. Franklin, my entire estate, including my interest in my uncle's, Jno. Armfield's estate, my shotgun, Winchester rifle, watch, goldheaded cane and everything that is mine. He is to have the interest arising from a proper investment of the money from my uncle's estate, to do with it as he pleases, but the principal is to go to his children in case he has any. In case he dies without heirs, I want my sister, Mrs. Adele Vanbibber, to have it on same condition. I want my brother, Edward N. Franklin, to qualify as my administrator and act without bond. I want him to buy a ticket to Louisville, Ky., for "Alice" and give her $500. J. A. Franklin.

The party spoken of as "Alice" was Armfield Franklin's mistress and she hailed from Louisville. Dr. John W. Franklin, father of the deceased, was the administer (ed. note: should be "administrator of the will") of his father-in-law (ed. note: should be "brother-in-law"), John Armfield, and this is why Dr. Ed. N. Franklin is bringing suit against him for the recovery of said property.

The will was not found until after fifteen years had elapsed after the death of Armfield Franklin, and was found in the gun-box by Dr. Ed. N. Franklin. An appeal will be taken to the Supreme Court.

The Daily American
Nashville, Tenn., Friday, February 27, 1891
Page 2
A Celebrated Lawsuit: Contest Over the Will of Armfield Franklin.
Brief History of the Circumstances Which Led to the Suit-Peculiar Hiding place of the Precious Document-Five Trials – The Supreme Court Decision.
Gallatin, Feb. 26.—(Special.)

—One of the most celebrated law suits that was ever in the courts at Gallatin was decided in the Supreme Court at Nashville yesterday. It was the famous will case of Franklin vs. Franklin, in which Dr. Ed. N. Franklin, of Gallatin, sues his father, Dr. John W. Franklin, for the recovery of a large estate left him by his brother, Armfield Franklin, who died in the fall of 1871 at Tallahassee, Fla.

The suit is not without its sensational features. Dr. John W. Franklin had three children by his first wife, who was a Miss Florida Noel, a daughter of Rev. Silas M. Noel, of Lexington, Ky., a distinguished Baptist minister in his day and the founder of Georgetown Ky., Male College. Three children were born to them, John

Armfield, Edward N. and Adele, the daughter, married a Mr. Van Bibber, of Belair, Md., a gentleman of wealth. John Armfield never married; Ed. N. married a Miss Hillman, of Nashville, the daughter of the wealthy iron merchant of that city. A brief history as to what led to this very celebrated will suit is as follows:

Some time after the close of the war, Armfield was employed as a drummer for a Louisville whisky house, and traveled in the South. During his stay in Louisville he fell in to the company of strange woman, who wound her toils about him. He fell a victim to the beautiful siren in the fall of 1871. She accompanied him to Georgia and Florida. She was represented as being married to him out of regard to the proprieties of life. Franklin died at Tallahassee, Fla., while on one of his trips. His effects consisted of a trunk and an English fowling piece, with its accoutrements. This was in November, 1871, over twenty years ago. The trunk and gun case were brought to Gallatin with the remains. The gun and case was in many hands after the death of Armfield.

One day Ed. was cleaning the gun, and turning the case upside down to get out the dust, a slip of paper fell out, which turns up to be the will of Armfield, This was sixteen years after Armfield's death. It devised to this brother Ed. his one-fifth interest in the estate of his uncle John Armfield to him. It further directed to pay Alice, his companion, $500, and to furnish her a ticket to Louisville, her home.

Ed. showed the will to his father, who was the administrator of the estate of John Armfield. The father protested and forgery was charged. A law suit against the father soon followed and a large number of witnesses examined to prove that the bill was genuine. Many said it was not the dead man's writing, others said it was.

One of the great arguments against setting up the will was that it was not found where wills are usually kept. On the other hand, it was argued that the dead man acted with great foresight in putting it under the plate of the gun case; that if it had been placed in the trunk Alice would have destroyed it, seeing she was left out, as it was not then known she was not his wife.

The suit has been tried five times, three times in the Circuit Court and twice in the Supreme Court. Ed Franklin has gained the suit every time a decision was reached. The suit involved thousands and thousands of dollars and interest for over sixteen years. The original estate was that of B. F. John Armfield, an uncle, who was a millionaire and a partner of the late Isaac Franklin, the owner of Fairview and of plantations and thousands of slaves in Louisiana. Thus ends the most celebrated will suit ever tried in these courts.

Barred recovery of the greater part of the estate, but recovery could be had of about $2500

The Courier Journal
Louisville, Kentucky, Friday, January 15, 1892
Barred by Limitation.
Nashville, Tenn., Jan. 14. — (Special.)

— The famous Franklin will case from Gallatin came up before the Supreme Court in a new phase, and was decided today. Dr. Ed. Franklin sued his father for the estate left him by his brother, Armfield Franklin, and the Supreme Court decided that the statute of limitation barred recovery of the greater part of the estate, but recovery could be had of about $2,500 that had passed into the old gentleman's hands within the past few years.

Reports of Cases Argued and Determined in the Supreme Court of Tennessee, Vol. VII
Nashville, TN 1892.
Printed by Marshall & Bruce. The court case of *Franklin v Franklin*. Pages 119-134.

Franklin v. Franklin.

(Nashville. January 14, 1892.)

1. COUNTY COURT. *Is Court of general jurisdiction as regards administration.*
Doctrine re-affirmed that the County Court is a Court of general jurisdiction as regards administration upon the estates of decedents; and that its proceedings had in administration cases are entitled to the protection of those rules and presumptions that obtain in favor of the judgments of Courts of general jurisdiction. *(Post, p. 128.)*
Case cited and approved: Railway Co. *v.* Mahoney, 89 Tenn., 311.

2. ADMINISTRATOR. *Appointment of voidable, not void, when.*
Appointment of administrator by County Court, upon the estate of a decedent as an intestate, is not void on collateral attack, but only voidable upon direct attack, where the decedent was not in fact an intestate, and his will was subsequently discovered and probated. *(Post, pp. 126-132.)*
Cases cited and approved: Pinkerton *v.* Walker, 3 Hay., 220; Baldwin *v.* Buford, 4 Yer., 20; Fay *v.* Reager, 2 Sneed, 200; Killebrew *v.* Murphy, 3 Heis., 551; Johnson v. Gaines, 1 Cold., 288; Railway Co. *v.* Mahoney, 89 Tenn., 311; 8 Cranch, 9; 14 Peters, 33.
Cited and distinguished: Wilson *v.* Frazier, 2 Hum., 30; D'Arusment *v.* Jones, 4 Lea, 251.

3. STATUTE OF LIMITATIONS. *Runs against decedents' estates, when.*
And statutes of limitations run against such administrator upon all causes of action that had accrued to the decedent; and where such administrator is barred, the executor, subsequently appointed upon discovery and probate of the will, is also precluded by that bar. *(Post, pp. 125-132.)*

4. SAME. *Ten years bars suit for legacy.*

Suit brought against an executor for recovery of a legacy more than ten years after final settlement of his accounts in the County Court is barred by the statute of limitations of ten years. *(Post, p. 132.)*
Code: 23473 (M. & V.); J2776 (T. & S.).

5. SAME. *Same. When settlement is final.*
In 1877 the executor made full and final settlement of his accounts in the County Court, showing amounts due the legatees or distributees. In 1885 he collected a claim from the Federal Government due the estate, which had not been taken into account in the former settlement. In regard to this latter sum he had made no settlement when he was sued as executor by the legatees in 1891.
Held: The settlement of 1877 was final in such sense that the statute of ten years began to run against legatees from its date, as to matters therein embraced, but not as to amount received by the executor in 1885. *(Post, pp. 122-125, 132.)*
Quiere: Did suit, *quia timet,* brought by claimants under will to impound and preserve the estate pending contest over probate of will, operate to arrest the running of statutes of limitations against them?
Case cited: Brown *v.* Brown, 14 Lea, 259.

6. SAME. *Six years bars suit for legacy, when.*
If an executor, after final settlement, appropriates the fund left in his hands to his own use, by some unequivocal act, upon the claim, made in good faith and under color, that he is the lawful legatee or distributee, then suit against him by the rightful legatee or distributee will be barred unless it is brought within six years after such appropriation of the fund by the executor. The statutes of three and ten years do not apply in such case. But this rule does not obtain in favor of an executor who has not made settlement or unequivocally appropriated the fund as distributee. *(Post, pp. 122-125.)*

7. WILL. *Example of class doctrine.*
Testator bequeathed to his brother, whom he nominated as his executor, his entire estate, including a legacy due testator from his uncle's estate. Testator then added: "He [the brother] is to have the interest arising from a proper investment of the money from my uncle's estate to do with as he pleases, but the principal is to go to his children in case he has any. In case he dies without heirs I want my sister * * * to have it on same conditions."
Held: The brother takes a life-time interest in the fund, and that upon his death his surviving children take the *corpus* as a class. *(Post, pp. 123-133, 134.)*
Cases cited and approved: Frierson *v.* Van Buren, 7 Yer., 606; Satterfield *v.* Mayes, 11 Hum., 58; Womack *v.* Smith, 11 Hum., 478; Bridgewater *v.* Gordon, 2 Sneed, 9.

FROM SUMNER.

Appeal from the Chancery Court of Sumner County. GEO. E. SEAY, Ch.
CHAS. R. HEAD, JAMES W. BLACKMORE, R. K. GILLESPIE, and T. C. MULLIGAN for Ed N. Franklin.

JAMES J. TURNER, S. F. WILSON, and B. D. BELL for J. W. Franklin.

SNODGRASS, J. This is a suit to recover the interest of John Armfield Franklin in the estate of John Armfield, who died testate, in Grundy County, Tennessee, in 1871, leaving a large personal estate to five legatees — testator's wife and four others. The widow dissented from the will, and took her interest under the law upon dissent, so that only the remainder of the estate was left to pass under the will. The four legatees entitled to it were the present complainants, Ed ET. Franklin, John Armfield Franklin, Mrs. A. Vanbibber, and Mrs. B. Archer. One of these, John Armfield Franklin, died in November, 1871. Ed N. Franklin was appointed and qualified as administrator of his estate December, 1876. John Armfield Franklin had, in fact, died testate, but his will was not discovered for many years thereafter, and not established, it being contested, until several years later — facts to be more particularly stated hereinafter.

The defendant, J. W. Franklin, was named as executor in the will of John Armfield. He qualified as such in the County Court of Grundy County October 2, 1871, and made a settlement of the estate with the Clerk of said Court July 30, 1875. In this settlement he was charged with $27,342.99 and credited with $12,209.54, leaving balance then in his hands of $15,133.45. On September 21, 1877, he made a final settlement, showing balance in his hands from former settlement, $15,133.45; collected since, $30,327.72; total, $45,4(31.77; credits since, $14,228 35; due distributees, $ 1,232.82. Amount due the widow of this sum was $10,410.94, leaving $20,821.88 to pass under the will, or $5,205.22 to each of the three living legatees, and the same amount to J. W. Franklin, who was the father and distributee of the dead one, John Armfield Franklin. This sum he kept as such distributee and appropriated. The remainder he paid to the parties already named entitled to it. All the parties acquiesced in the settlement, and the present complainant gave his receipt for balance in full due him under it December 24, 1877.

In January, 1885, Defendant J. W. Franklin, as executor of John Armfield, collected a claim of his testator's estate against the United States Government of $18,000, which, after deducting executor's compensation and attorney's fees paid for its collection, and paying the widow, left in his hands for distribution the sum of $1,890 for each living legatee and the distributee of John Armfield Franklin. He appropriated this $1.890 as such distributee, and he also applied the same amount due Ed N. Franklin on debts which he held against Ed X. Franklin. The other legatees he paid in full.

In the meanwhile, about the time of the collection and disposition of this fund, a will of John Armfield Franklin was found. This will, which we quote for the purpose of construction hereinafter, is as follows:

"WASHINGTON, GA., October, 1871.
"This is my last will and testament. I will and bequeath to my brother, Edward N. Franklin, my entire estate, including my interest in my Uncle John Armfield's estate, my shotgun, Winchester rifle, watch, gold-headed cane, and every thing that is mine. He is to have the interest arising from a proper investment of the money from my uncle's estate, to do with as he pleases, but the principal is to go to his children in

case he has any. In case he dies without heirs, I want my sister, Mrs. Adele Vanbibber, to have it on same conditions. I appoint my brother, Ed N. Franklin, to qualify as my administrator and act without bond. I want him to buy a ticket to Louisville, Ky., for Alice and give her $500.

"J. A. FRANKLIN."

It was offered for probate at the April term, 1885, of the County Court of Sumner County, was contested, and finally established as the will and ordered probated, and admitted to probate April 13, 1891, in the County Court, under decree of this Court pronounced March 6, 1891. When the will was admitted to probate Ed N. Franklin qualified as executor. On April 28, 1891, he procured an order of the County Court annulling and revoking his appointment as administrator of the estate of John Armfield Franklin, which had been made, as before recited, on December 28, 1876.

Before this will was admitted to probate, Ed N. Franklin, in his own name, and as next friend of his minor children, legatees under the discovered will, filed a bill *quia timet,* alleging facts of discovery and pending contest of the will of John Armfield Franklin, and seeking to bring the executor of John Armfield to a settlement. This bill was filed March 24, 1890.

After the will was admitted to probate, and on April 29, 1891, he filed an amended and supplemental bill as executor of said will, and as next friend of said minors, for same purpose—that is, to compel settlement by the executor, and to recover the distributive share of John Armfield Franklin in John Armfield's estate, which, as we have before seen, had been received and appropriated by J. W. Franklin as distributee of the estate of his deceased and supposed intestate son.

The defense was the statute of limitations of three, six, and ten years. By cross-bill defendant also sought to have his own claims against Ed N. Franklin set off against any recovery Ed N. might show himself entitled to as legatee of John Armfield Franklin.

Whether the first bill *quia timet* can be considered as arresting from date of its filing the statute of limitations, as intimated such a bill might do in the case of *Brown* v. *Brown,* 14 Lea, 259, and thereby make it in time to save the bar of the statute of six years, if J. W. Franklin must be treated as having held the $1,890 as distributee and not as executor since it was received in January, 1885, the Court deems it unnecessary to decide, though it does decide that six and not three years is the least time that could bar such action. By the majority so determining, the Court also holds that, sued as executor who had made final settlement in 1877, but none as to the last money of the estate received in January, 1885, the only statute which could be applicable in his favor was that of ten years. The question is whether that can be relied on as to final settlement of 1877. The Chancellor held it could not, and defendant appealed.

The theory upon which it is now insisted by complainant that this statute did not run, is that the appointment of Ed N. Franklin as administrator of estate of John Armfield Franklin in 1876 was *void,* and that, therefore, there was no one capable of suing until the appointment and qualification of the executor in 1891.

The first appointment is assumed to be void because John Armfield Franklin did not die *intestate,* and it is insisted that the County Court therefore had no jurisdiction to appoint an administrator. If the contention be true that the appointment was void, then the statute did not run. If the appointment was valid—if only *voidable*—the statute did run; and this is the main question in the case. The appointment was not void. This question is not an open one in this State. *Pinkerton* v. *Walker*, 3 Haywood, 220; *Baldwin* v. *Buford*, 4 Yer., 20.

In England, at common law, the rule prevailed that an appointment of an administrator by the ordinary, made in derogation of the right of an executor qualified or acting with or without probate of the will (for there he could do almost all the acts incident to his office except some relating to suits before probate: 1 Williams on Executors, top paging 338-347, 6th Am. Ed.), or who had not renounced the trust, or from whom the will had been concealed (by party obtaining letter, as explained by Judge Freeman in dissenting opinion in *Brown* v. *Brown*, 14 Lea, 383) was void. 'See Williams, on Executors, Vol. I., Book 6, Ch. 3, top page 655, 6th Am. Ed.

The rule was recognized at least to the full extent in case of an appointment where there were living executors appointed and qualified and capable of acting, in two cases in the Supreme Court of the United States. *Griffith* v. *Frazier*, 8 Cranch, 9 (Lawyers' Co-op. Ed., Book 3, p. 471); *Kane* v. *Paul*, 14 Peters, 33 (Lawyers' Co-op. Ed., Book 10, p. 341).

But in the former it was distinctly recognized as the rule that if a Court grant administration where there is an executor who has not qualified, its act, though erroneous, is valid until repealed (pages 25, 26), and the latter refers to this case as authority. Both are digested as deciding this principle by legitimate deduction in the Indexed Digest of Supreme Court Reports, Vol. I., p. 793.

Here there is no cause for the application of the English doctrine of "concealment" if the entire rule on that subject prevailed in this State, because there was no pretense that the will was concealed by defendant or any one else.

But in the 4 Yerger case already cited Judge Catron points out the distinction between the executor's right derived almost exclusively from the will under the English law, and his right under our law as affected by statute, and shows the English rule so 'founded not applicable here (pages 19, 20, 21). And the distinction is further elaborated in *Fay* v. *Reager*, 2 Sneed, 200, and *Killebrew* v. *Murphy*, 3 Heis., 551; the latter case probably going too far in assuming the existence of certain power in the executor in advance of qualification, though the power did exist in the same person as widow, and hence the case was on this point correct upon its facts.

Under our law the County Court is a Court of general and exclusive jurisdiction on the subject of administration; and when it makes an appointment of an administrator on the estate of a deceased resident of this State, the appointment is valid until revoked.

Residence in a given county, like intestacy, is made a requisite of the power to appoint, and it has been said an appointment made by the County Court of a county in which a deceased had no residence at time of death is *void*. *Wilson* v. *Frazier*, 2 Hum., 30.

But the term was inaccurately used for *voidable*, for the Court, in the very case in which it was used, held that it was only voidable, and that to adjudge it void there must be a contest in the Court where made; and this exact point was afterward decided in the case of *Johnson* v. *Gaines, ExW,* 1 Cold., 288, and again explicitly determined in the case of *Railroad Company* v. *Mahoney,* 5 Pickle, 811.

There it was said that the County Court was authorized to determine for itself the existence of the facts which authorized the appointment, and, having done so, the appointment was not void. Page 318.

It is true that in that case there was no question of intestacy, and the question was one of residence or inhabitancy, arid the principle was not extended there beyond the ease of an admitted intestate; but intestacy, like inhabitancy, is one of the facts the County Court must determine, and the two questions fall together within the power of the Court to settle when the appointment of an administrator is asked. When the appointment is made, both are adjudged, and that is conclusive until reversed or vacated. *Schluter* v. *Bank,* Lawyers' Reports, Annotated, Book 5, pages 513, 514, and authorities cited.

In the Schluter case, which was a well-considered one where many authorities were referred to in argument and by the Court, the Court said: "Our attention has been called to no case, and we are confident that none can be found, holding that the subsequent discovery of a will, and its admission to probate, renders the prior appointment of an administrator absolutely void, so as to give no protection to persons who in dealing with the administrator have acted on the faith thereof." Page 513, citing further Woerner on Administration, pages 568, 571, 588.

It would have been more nearly correct, if not absolutely so, to have said: "No modern case can be found so holding." See also 4 Ohio, 138; 58 Maine, 225; 31 Maine, 504.

Like intestacy, as we have seen, the question of residence has been treated as a jurisdictional one, and there are cases cited in the books in which it has been held that finding it incorrectly by the Court authorized to make the appointment, rendered the appointment void. There were a number of these cases in Massachusetts. See cases collected in 1 Williams on Executors, top page 631, 6 Am. Ed., note C.

But the rule is now changed in that State by statute to meet the hardship involved in such a judicial view *(Ibid.),* and specially opinion in *Record* v. *Howard,* 58 Maine, 225.

The only apparent qualification of that doctrine (for it is not really so) is the appointment of an administrator on the estate of a living man, for this is universally held void, and that upon the ground that no Court is vested with such jurisdiction. *Railroad Company* v. *Moloney,* 5 Pickle, 319; *Moore* v. *Smith,* 73 Am. Dec, 122, and notes; 47 Am. Hep., 458, and notes; 107 111., 517.

Death is the one fact which must exist to give any Court jurisdiction. When it exists the others of residence and intestacy are open to proof. If decided erroneously the appointment may be voidable, but is not void. One Court went to the extent of holding that erroneous ascertainment of this fact did not make such an appointment void. But subsequently the same Court held that appointment void, it appearing that the Court in fact had not received evidence of it. *Roderigas* v. *East River Savings Institution,* 32 Am. Rep., 309 *(N. Y.).*

When the question first arose in this State, it was by a divided Court that it was settled adversely to the validity of such appointment where the fact of death was found incorrectly in the appointment. 4 Lea, 251. But it is obvious from that case that such fact was the only one the non-existence of which would render such appointment absolutely *void*.

To the same effect, as the question is now settled that the action of the County Court making the appointment is only voidable and not void, are the cases of *Varnell* v. *League,* 9 Lea, 158; *Posey* v. *Eaton,* 9 Lea, 504; *Brown* v. *Brown,* 14 Lea, 253; *State* v. *Anderson,* 16 Lea, 321.

There were three cases determined together in the last opinion. The facts of all are not given, but among the cases in which Anderson's appointment was held not void was one in which there was a will naming an executor. No distinction was taken as to the validity or invalidity of Anderson's appointment as administrator on this account, because, though the question was made, the Court held that none existed. Counsel cite other unreported cases to same effect.

We think no question is better settled in this State, and in the current of modern authority, or upon sounder reason. Wills may frequently be made and lie, as this, for years without discovery. The exercise of the jurisdiction of appointment of an administrator would be always unsafe and uncertain if the appointment was to be rendered void *ab initio* by the discovery of a will. The evils attendant upon such a rule are far greater than can possibly result from the contrary holding. It were better that rights thus acquired should be settled by the statute of limitations than that parties should never acquire any in cases of administration, or never be sure that those supposed to have been acquired were in fact so.

The old English rule to the contrary was in 1857 changed there by statute 20 and 21 Victoria, Chapter 77, Section 75, cited in 1 Williams on Executors, 6th American Edition, pages 619, 632, 680. And so it is generally changed where it ever prevailed in the American States by effect of statutes making executor's power depend on Court appointment and qualification. 7 Am. & Eng. Ency. of Law, p. 193, and notes; 1 Williams on Executors, top page 347, and notes, 6th Am. Ed.

The settlement made in 1877 was final in the sense of the statute, notwithstanding years after another claim due the estate, not therein included, was collected by the executor; and suit to recover balance due in that settlement could not be sustained after ten years. As neither bill in this cause was filed within ten years of that date, no recovery can be had on that account. The money received in January, 1885, was within ten years of the filing of either bill, and recovery, therefore, can be had as to the $1,890 due as John Armfield Franklin's proportion of that fund.

The complainant will therefore, as executor of John Armfield Franklin, recover this amount with interest from the date it came to the hands of defendant as executor of John Armfield. He will recover interest because there was nothing to prevent a payment of that fund at that time, as there was a party in existence capable of receiving it — the representative of John Armfield Franklin's estate.

After it is received, complainant, as legatee, has an interest, but what that interest is can only be ascertained after settlement of expenses of the estate incurred in litigation—it seems there are no debts or other charges against the estate. But it is obvious that large expenses have been incurred in establishing the will and prosecuting this cause, and it is only out of the net surplus that the legacy is to be settled. Of whatever this may be, complainant will be entitled to a life estate, and defendant to a set-off as to this, on account of his debts established as decreed by the Chancellor.

The corpus of the fund remaining after settlement of expenses and charges indicated, will, on the expiration of the life estate of Ed N. Franklin, belong to his surviving children, who take as a class under the will, the bequest being to a class of persons subject to fluctuation by increase or diminution of its number in consequence of future births or deaths, and the time of payment or distribution of such fund being fixed at a subsequent period on the happening of a designated event, and the bequest being of an aggregate fund given to the children as a unit and passing a joint interest. 7 Yer., 606; 11 Hum., 58, 478; 2 Sneed, 9.

The word "heirs" used in the will is manifestly used in the sense of children.

The cause will be remanded for an account to ascertain the amount, if any, which may be the subject of set-off in favor of defendant.

The costs of the cause accrued below will be paid two-thirds by defendant and one-third by complainant; that of this Court will be equally divided between them, both having appealed and assigned errors. The amount charged to complainant may be paid out of the fund recovered to be administered.

Appendix 2

Selected Newspaper Ads and Articles
Relevant to Beersheba Springs from 1871

These articles provide an image of the resort community of Beersheba Springs, Tennessee at the time Edward was writing his letters to Nannie. Some are informative, and some are highly entertaining, particularly the two describing the Grand Masque Ball that Edward speaks of. The last article is a flowery eulogy for slave trader John Armfield published in the paper after his death in 1871. This is followed by a rebuttal essay on my part entitled, "Legacy." The essay is meant as a contribution to the modern-day, slavery reconciliation conversation.

Nashville Union and American
Nashville, Tenn., Saturday, May 13, 1871
Beersheba Springs, Grundy County, Tenn.

   This property having been purchased by the undersigned, and thoroughly refitted and furnished, will be opened to the public for the ensuing season on the 15th June next.
   For the benefit of those persons who have never visited this, before the war, celebrated Watering Place, we beg leave to say that for the excellency of its Chalybeate and Freestone Waters, grandeur of scenery and purity of atmosphere, it is not surpassed, if equaled, by any similar establishment in the South. The location is upon one of the highest points of the Cumberland Mountains, within a few hours' ride of the University of the South, and of the large Swiss Colony recently established in this State.
   Visitors leaving Huntsville, Chattanooga or Nashville by the morning train will arrive at the Springs, via Tullahoma and McMinnville, on the evening of the same day.
   Parties wishing to engage rooms for the season, can do so by addressing us at Nashville until 15th May, after that time at Beersheba Spring.

Charges for Board.
By the Day $3: by the Week $17.50: by the Month
$60. Children and servants, half price.
Resident Physicians.
Dr. J. D. Winston, of Nashville; Dr. E. N. Franklin,
of Sumner county.
my2 2w B   S. M. SCOTT & CO.

(Editor's note: the above recurring ad appeared in several newspapers throughout the South that year.)

The Columbia Herald
Columbia, Tenn., July 28, 1871
Beersheba Springs

     Before the war, Beersheba had become one of the cherished institutions of our Southern people. Its beautiful and magnificent location on the mountains, easy (sic) of access and in the most pleasant and delightful climate on the continent, with its unsurpassed accommodations, very naturally made it a popular and charming resort for the people of the South who were forced during the Summer months to seek refuge in more healthful climes. The war in its march of destruction left this beautiful place stripped of everything except the bare buildings. Last season it was reopened for the first time; and this season, under the management of Sam. M. Scott, it has regained its former renown, and offers the public every comfort and accommodation to be had at a watering place. It is furnished in excellent style and the accommodations are unsurpassed. Already a large crowd from Louisiana, Mississippi, Alabama, Texas, Georgia and Tennessee, are in attendance.

     It is, in all respects, the most inviting and delightful summer resort on the continent. It is easy of access, being only a few hours ride over a pleasant road and fine coaches, from the beautiful town of McMinville (sic). Passengers from Nashville and Chattanooga, reach there the same day.

Republican Banner
Nashville, Tenn., August 13, 1871
The Grand Bal Masque Last Thursday Night

Beersheba, August 11, 1871:

     The grand masquerade ball at Beersheba, concerning which not a little has been written, and a vast deal said—which has been the absorbing topic agitating the feminine hearts of the angels of this paradise in the clouds for a fortnight past—which has been looked forward to with eager expectancy and fond anticipations for many days, rendering the dear enchantresses so nervous that they could scarcely keep the count of their "runs" in the ten pin alley, or keep from striking their own dear little gaiters with croquet mallets—the grand ball—the ball *par excellence* of the Beersheba season—*Un Ballo en Maschera Splenderissimo*, is now in the full tide of a brilliant and happy success.

     And the night is far spent even to the "sma' hours ayant the twal," entirely too late for the ghost of a hope to reach you e the morrow's mail, so this will probably de deferred to your Sunday's issue.

     But on the presumption that at least a portion of your city readers will be interested in a brief history of the affair, and that everybody at Beersheba will certainly be curious to know what the papers have to say about it, the postponement will not necessarily rule it out of order.

     A full orchestra is just now discoursing a waltz.—*Il Bacio*—in the ball-room, and a dozen couples are whirling to its inspiring measure—so that this epistle cannot be voted literally out of time, no matter how "lamely and unfashionable" the halt in its gait.

The ball-room is tastefully decorated with festoons of evergreen and flower baskets pendant from the ceiling, over which a brilliant chandelier in the center and hundreds of miniature wall tapers shed a soft romantic light. The floor is thronged with dancers in every imaginable variety of costume—for not only has Loiseau's *costumier* been called into requisition, but Kirkpatrick's mountain dry goods house, and the ingenuity of the ladies have been taxed to their utmost capacity in supplying the wardrobes. The result would do credit to a carnival of the Creole Mardi-gras, or a *fete* night at the *Mabile*. The dresses are exceedingly tasteful, and the masquerades rich and elegant in the extreme. The assertion may be safely ventured that a more bewildering galaxy of beauty, a finer collection of rare and radiant maidens, in more captivating attire, is not to be witnessed at a fashionable water-place more than once in a season. It is somewhat difficult in such a kaleidoscopic array of characters to follow them all, even with the aid of two or three lady mentors, who know them by heart. But let us do the best we can to give your city readers a more intelligent idea of the situation. Miss Lizzie Elder, of Murfreesboro, was dressed as Spanish Noblesse, orange satin train, black lace draperies and diamond crown and necklace. Miss Bessie McCrea, of Nashville, as an Indian Princess, a gorgeous dress of rainbow satin and jewels. Miss Maggie McCrea as the "Tennessee-Touch-me-not," Brussells lace and diamonds. Miss Eliza Winston, Gulnare, blue satin, gold lace, velvet joupe and corsage with jewels and lace. Miss Winston, Aurora, white silk train, olive and pink illusion over-dress, veil and draperies, jeweled star and coronet; Miss Lulu Winston, Wood Nmph (sic), white tarletan, trimmings of fruit leaves and ferns; Miss Mannie Porter, evening dress, train of blue silk, point lace and diamonds; Miss Georgia Woods, Black Lyons silk, train, with overskirt and trimmings of rose colored satin, hair a Pompadour with powder and French roses; Miss Annie Porter, of Nashville, tarletan, train, couleurde rose, point applique, and diamonds; Mrs. Maggie Evans, pink tarletan, jewels and lace; Miss Sallie Evans, as Purity, in white tarletan with white ribbons and flowers. Miss Annie Hollins, as a Goddess of the Rainbow—white tarletan—rainbow mid ruches, and coronet of pearls. Miss Porter Hollins—La Fille du Regiment, dress Vivandiere. Miss Burton, of Murfreesboro, Gipsy Queen. Miss Lit Lindsley, of Nashville, in blue silk, Paris muslin over-dress. Miss Cooper, of Nashville, white tarletan and pearls. Miss Schluter, of Nashville, as Night, in a black tarletan dress and veil, spangled with jeweled crown. Miss Barrows, of Mississippi, as Innocence, in white tarletan and flowing train, Miss Freeland, of Mississippi, in white illusion and French roses. Miss Perkins, of Mississippi, white muslin with pink trimmings and Valenciennes lace. Miss Murfree, of Nashville, dress of white silk, trimming of point lace and satin; Miss Mollie Chadwell, as Venus, in white illusion with spangled crown of stars and zone; Miss Emma Chadwell, silk train, Metternich green, point lace and pearls; Miss Sallie Hayes, Nashville, yellow silk, black velvet overdress and corsage with gold lace and crimson velvet trimmings and jewels; Miss Rebecca Correy, of Nasvile, white Paris muslin, fluted ruffles, white lace. Miss Theo. Branch, and Mrs. Partington; Miss Alathea Allison and Miss Jennie Allin in lovely toilettes of light mourning; and Miss Mary Kirkman and Miss Mary Woods: pink and white dresses with crushed roses; Miss Olah Hicks, of Franklin, in a pretty dress of white and green; Miss Thomas, as Cinderella, and quite a number of others whose names and characters and dresses it was impossible to obtain. Among the gentlemen, the following characters were noticeable: Mr. Coldwell as the Prince of Como; Dr. E. N. Franklin as Don Cesar de Bazan; Dr. Jamison as Prince Lavender; Mr. M. Moore as the Knight of the Golden Cross; Colonel C. A. Sheafe as the Black Prince; Mr. Gardner as an Arab Boy; Mr. Handly as the Swiss Brigand; Mr. Robert Ewing as Prince Leander; Mr. George Gray as Richelieu; Mr. Wilson as "Gen. McMackin;" Mr. Jo. Brown as a Rustic Mountaineer, and a number of beautiful little Misses as fairies and naiads, with little boys as sailors and harlequins.

Among the grotesque impersonations, Mr. Fuller's "Girl of the Period," Mr. Foster's "Widow in Weeds," and Mr. Wilson's "Gen. McMackin," were infinitely amusing. The removal of the masks occasioned great merriment as the characters were revealed to each other. The spectators seemed to enjoy the fun as much as the chief actors themselves. The wall-flowers were numerous—including old folks and bachelors of an uncertain age, and, of course, married gentlemen without their families, who could not in the absence of their *cara sposas* be persuaded to dance for any consideration. There were present, also, a large number of the native from the valleys and mountains adjacent, whose fresh and innocent bewilderment at the spectacle was infinitely amusing.

By no means the least interesting feature of the occasion was the grand banquet—an impromptu enterprise on the part of Mr. Scott, the proprietor, in the highest degree creditable to that excellent gentleman and his industrious hotel staff. It was a very sumptuous repast of the choicest viands, cakes and fruits, served in inimitable style, and winning golden opinion from everybody. After supper the dancing was resumed, and a hundred twinkling feet are now skipping to the exhilarating influences of "Shoo Fly" in the adjacent apartment, and the table on which this is scribbled, sways as if a small sized earthquake was trying its muscle on the mountain. As to how long the festivities will be kept up, it would be hazardous to predict, from the spirit which seems now to possess the dancers. The indications are that the slanting beams of to-morrow's sun will come into competition with the lingering tapers, and light the gay masqueraders to their matutinal couches, when this historian will have wandered far down the steep of Beersheba heights toward the valley and the Happy Fishing Ground of the Faithful—leaving behind him as sociable and happy a little community as was every collected together, but carrying with him the pleasant reminiscences of as delightful a week's recreation as rarely falls to the lot of the noble army of martyrs whom the Gods have sentenced for life to the midnight lamp and the tireless quill. But for all that, here's perpetuity to Beersheba! Fairy land, home of the dutiful, beautiful—long be remembered its legends and loves. And when next it holds its Summer session, may we be there to see!

Nashville Union and American
Nashville, Tenn., Tuesday, August 15, 1871
The Mask Ball a Grand and Brilliant Affair

To the Editors of the Union and American:

The guests of these famous Springs understand why they are here, and keep alive the interest of enjoyment of engaging in every kind of amusement conducive to health and to kill monotony. The great event of the season was witnessed by your correspondent in the large hall of the magnificent hotel here, in a grand and successful masquerade ball, in which both old and young participated with wholesome zest, and who were determined to make it *the masque* of the many different summer resorts and springs of the South.

At about 9 o'clock, the hall being brilliantly lighted, the maskers commenced their actions, coming in by twos and threes, and singly, until some sixty were gathered upon the floor. The splendid music from Bush's band threw their feet to tripping the "light fantastic," and gave them eloquent motion in all their movements. The comical ones afforded laughter for the lookers-on and dignified others. All the characters were well sustained, and all was as well done as the best critic could desire. Beautifully prominent among the glittering lady characters, was Miss Eliza Winston representing "Gulnare," of Byron's corsair. Her costume was indeed pretty with its bright spangles and many colored silks and fringes. The "Indian Princess, by Miss Bessie McCrea, was excellently take, and her long dark hair, and sparkling eyes even after the unmasking, proved how beautiful she was, lighted up with the colors so loved by the tawny race of which she was a representative. The large crescent shaped ring hung in the nose of her mask, made her look aboriginal indeed. The "Tennessee Touch-me-not," was a warning to many gallants, and it was impossible for her to keep them from showing her much admiration and attention. Miss Maggie McCrea in this character, was dressed in white tarletan puffed with pink, and with a flowing lace veil covered with touch-me-nots and reaching to the floor. As after the shower come the Promise sign of the Flood, a beautiful "Rainbow," represented by Miss Annie Hollins, dressed in colored tarletans, placed alternately so well blended, that is (sic) was impossible to keep from gazing in rapt admiration. Then Miss Sa__ie (ed. note: could be Sadie or Sallie) Sluters (sic. ed. note: should be Schluter) as "Night," Starry night, a moon wearing a crown of brilliant stars, and without a cloud, came with mellow light, followed immediately by beautiful "Aurora," by Miss Jennie Winston. Tinted with the hues of early morning in a flowing veil-cloud over white and blue with spangles, she heralded the approach of "Morning," represented by Miss Mollie Chadwell, dressed in white tarletan, with crown and veil, covered with golden stars. These two characters were, indeed, beautiful. As gorgeous as is the departure of the sun after doing service for us here, the western horizon was never of more splendor than appeared Miss Annie Porter, dressed in bright colors, representing "Sunset." In the soft twilight, and wafted by zephyrs, came Miss Lula Winston as the "Mountain Goddess," or "Queen Mab," whose illusion dress was covered with fruit, flowers and forest leaves, made her look irresistible. With her were the golden-winged "Faries," (sic) Willie and Maggie Hollins and Annie Thomas, whose brightness reflected in varied beauty the color of early evening.

In all the spirit of those of whom she was a representative, Miss Lizzie Elder, of Memphis, appeared as a Spanish lady of nobility, dressed in a yellow satin, with a black lace head dress flowing from a high corral set in true spanish fashion, and completing perfectly her features, complexion, color of eyes and hair for this especial character. Gen MacMacklin Wilson, also once of Spain's domain, was entirely captivated. Seeking to discover the future, and reading the past from the palm of the hand, Miss Annie Burton, as the "Mountain Fortune Teller," freely ventured amongst the maskers and decided the fate of many of them. She was dressed in a beautiful orange colored velvet, with black velvet hearts, and trimmed with silver braid. The soldier's pride and friend of the sick and wounded, "the Daughter of the Regiment,' by Miss Porter Hollins, presented her canteen and done many offices in a true soldierly manner. Her scarlet skirt, black coat and red cap, trimmed with gold, made her look romantic and interesting. Miss Sallie Hays, with her happy smiles and pleasant recognitions for all, brought into the ballroom the brightness of color so characteristic of the oriental clime from whence she was, and scattered a genial rariance (sic) over all present. Her dress was made of buff, with black velvet outskirt trimmed with gold lace and red velvet. Her feathered cap set jauntily, captivated many a beau. Miss Olah Hicks of Franklin, as the "Wood Nymph, fresh from the forest groves and nooks, decked with dew that shone as diamonds, and with green leaves and gold, assisted the Kattydids (sic) in their songs, and rivalled the fireflies. "Our Grandmother," by Miss Theola Branch, called from all that reverence due old age, and her sweet appearance roused up feelings of real love and respect. Katie Massengale was sweet looking as a little Tamborine (sic) Girl. Her beautiful head-dress of different colored ribbons crossed on white Swiss, gave her an exquisite finish. Ladie Massengale, as "the Posteria Dancing Girl" was an attraction.

"Mrs Partington," by Mrs. Larcomb, with her "which" drolleries, old time actions and dress, was the main feature of the mask among the lady characters. She was up to all the items of to-day only in her misinterpretations, though in the midst of these interests her son Ike, (Joe Brown,) required her car. He would declare that the one who made the most noise was the best dancer, and continually worried the old lady into fidgets by some ridiculous mischievousness. She says that she was the bell of the *bal masque*, and that "Ike was the *beller*, for he did make sich a noise."

Fastidiously walking and acting, and making herself conspicuous thereby, was the "Girl of the Period," whose panier, three feet in diameter, and chignon, made up of three large ones, attracted much attention. Her white tarletan trail was at least five feet long, and the way she tossed her head, decorated with a nobby hat set jauntily, and her magnificent form and step, were a caution to ladies, and completely won the admiration of all the young men. Her real name was Andrew J. Fulier. "Miss Stimmons" was a "wictim" of false love, and therefor was a "widow in weeds." Will Foster was dressed in this character, with a black dress, veil and hat. Capt. Chas. Sheafe was a "Black Prince," dressed in black velvet, spangled with silver. Dr. Ned. (ed. note: Edward) Franklin's "Don Ceasar" (sic) was an elegant costume. Nat. Gardner took the character of an "Arab Boy. His was a beautiful silk bloomer dress, with spangles and lace. The "red Knight was represented by Alfred Moore, of Manchester. W. B. Coldwell, as Prince Como, looked exceedingly fine. "Macheallewakiskedealambumfam," the "Big Ingun," by Ei. Buford, would fool the verieat (sic) detective of the tawny tribe, when dressed in leather, beads, feathers and paint, as he was on this occasion. Ross Handley wore a magnificent "Swiss Brigand's" dress, and looked for all the world as though he could have kidnapped a pile of gold and taken a beautiful girl as a ransom. Bob Ewing, as "Prince Leander," was particularly favored by the glittering lady characters, for his graceful movements and dancing, and his silk costume, merited their admiration and attention. There is only one General McMackin in the world, but Col. B. F. Wilson, President Mechanics Bank, Nashville, aspired to the honor of being a second, and accordingly dressed himself in the long spotted robe and hat of the real general, took his gait, and mixed among the crowd just as familiarly. G. S. Gray, who will open the Masonic Hall, at Nashville, with a theatrical company from Chicago, in October, personated "Richelieu," and "Charles II, King of Spain." He knows how to do it. The "Wild Irishman" ranted and cavoorted (sic) extensively, to the enjoyment of everybody, Mr. E. F. Flemming, of Manchester, was this native of the "ould sod." Addison Hays, of Memphis, as the "man in Black" contrasted with L. Q. Jeffries, as the "Man in White." Masters Lawrence and Coldwell and Dixie Doulass (ed. note: possibly meant to be Douglass) were active "Sailor Boys," and deserve credit for their acting.

The unmasking created considerable merriment, for, as is always the case, you always guess wrongly, and many were deceived. The comical ones were the quietest upon other occasions, and vice versa. After the unmasking, all repaired to a sumptuous repast prepared by the generous hosts, and all were well satisfied and profuse in their praises. Pyramids of cake, and jelly glasses, and baskets of fruit and candies, ornamented the tables.

All the guest of the Springs were at the "masque." Little and big folks alike enjoyed it, and all were satisfied. The dancing lasted until away past the "wee sma hours," and gradually the party decreased, leaving a vacant hall.

The Examiner
Gallatin, Tenn., Saturday, August 19, 1871
Beersheba Springs
(Correspondence Examiner)

Beersheba Springs, now the most celebrated and popular watering place in the South, may be almost claimed as a Sumner County institution, as it was through the enterprize (sic) and liberality of one of our former citizens, Col. Jno. Armfield, that the property was improved and brought into public notice. Col. Armfield in 1855 purchased the property, and with the view of making it the watering place of the South, improved it on an immense scale, erecting fine buildings and making every improvement necessary to its success. He spent over $100,000 in this work, and when the war broke out, it had been made a grand success. Col. Armfield built for himself a handsome summer residence, where he at present spends the summer months. He sold the hotel property to a Company in 1859, who managed it until the war. During the war the property was considerably damaged and the company broken up, and in consequence of their condition, nothing was done with the Springs until last season, when they were purchased by some gentlemen of Nashville, and opened under the management of Mrs. I. C. Nicholson of the Nicholson House. She undertook the work under many disadvantages, but made it, under all the circumstances, a success. The present season it passed into the hands of Sam. M. Scott, for many years the popular proprietor of the Nashville City Hotel. Mr. Scott has the Hotel in thorough repair, the rooms neatly and elegantly furnished, and the table, the best of any hotel in the South. Under his excellent management its ancient renown has been re-established and its former popularity restored.

Beersheba is the most charming and delightful summer resort on the Continent. It is located on the Cumberland mountain, 3000 feet above the level of the sea, in the most delightful climate in the world. The water is chalybeate and freestone, gushing forth as clear as chrystal (sic) and is of a most delightful temperature, and the chalybeate possesses medicinal qualities of great value.

Mr. Scott has been fortunate in securing the assistance of the renowned Gen. T. C. McMackin, the Autocrat of hotel keepers of the South. He knows how to please everybody and to make everybody feel at home and enjoy themselves. He is the beloved "grandpa" of all the children.

Beersheba is surrounded by a large number of neat, tasty and elegant cottages that are occupied during the season. Before the war they were built by citizens from different parts of the South. Judge Morgan, of Louisiana, built a magnificent establishment at a cost of some $15_____(ed. note: unclear, possibly "hundred") owned and occupied by Mr._____. _____ (ed. note: names unclear) F. Kenner, Col. Dick Bell, Col. John M. Bass, Dr. T. J. Harding, General Dahlgreen, Col. Phillips, Bishop Polk, Bishop Otey, Col. Sumner, Rolfe S. Saunders, and a great many others had cottages there before the war. Since then, most of them have changed ownership. A. J. Porter, W. J. Murfree and W. L. Brown, of Nashville, Maj. A. D. Banks, of Mississippi, Col. John Armfield, Rolfe S. Saunders and several others, with their families, occupy cottages this season. Among the visitors are Judge Wm. Yerger and family, Judge John M. Lea and family, Gen. Humes and family, Col. John W. Burton and family, Albert Frierson and family, Duncan E. Frierson, Judge Barrow, Duncan F. Carter and family, Thos. D. Craighead and family, Gen. A. Smith and family, of Mississippi, Col. S. W. Hicks and family, Albert Roberts, the genial gentleman and gifted journalist, Col. J. B. Killebrew, of the *Union and American*, Col. A. J. Kelar, the Marshal Ney of the Tennessee press, Col. B. F. Wilson and a large number of gentlemen.

Among the ladies are the elegant and Imperial Mrs. Gen. John H. Morgan (*nee* Ready); the charming and beautiful Miss Nannie Hillman, of Nashville; the Misses McCrea, Winston, O'Bryan, Evans, Buck, Woods; Mrs. Elliston, Mrs. Leech, Mrs. Burton, Thomas, Mrs. Lee, Mrs. McWhirter, Cunningham, Pilcher, Nichol, Hollins, Carter, Douglass, and Miss Mannie Porter, R. Corry, Elder, Schluter, Burton, Kirkman, Allison, Brown and countless others. With such a crowd how could it be otherwise than delightful beyond any conception short of reality!

Beersheba is in the midst of one of the finest fruit regions in the country. The winter apples are unsurpassed. The grape flourishes finely, and it is the opinion of those skilled in the grape culture that this climate and locality is far superior to any place in American save the golden shores of California. Pears, peaches and cherries also do well. Vegetables grow finely, especially Irish potatoes. It is the best place for sheep raising this side of Texas. This bench of Cumberland mountain is the natural sheep walk of North America. Coal abounds in numberless mines of inexhaustible supply and superior quality. So it will be seen Beersheba is a great place. It is situated 18 miles from McMinnville and about 18 miles from Tracey City, affording two routes to passengers. Persons leaving Nashville and Chattanooga by the morning train, reach Beersheba the same evening to tea, and returning, reach Nashville the same day of leaving to dinner.

A brilliant wedding was celebrated at Beersheba last week. Miss Adele Franklin, daughter of our respected and well know fellow-citizen, Dr. John Franklin, was married at the residence of her uncle, Col. Jno. Armfield, to Geo. L. Van Bibber, a talented and promising young member of the Baltimore bar. It was a most magnificent affair, rivalling the good old times that distinguished our country before the war. Mrs. Armfield surpassed herself in getting up the wedding supper, and was truly elegant, eliciting the praise of all who were present on the happy occasion.

Nashville Union and American
Nashville, Tenn., Sunday, September 24, 1871
Gen. John Armfield.

The many friends and acquaintances of this well-known gentleman will be pained to learn of his demise, after a protracted illness, on the 20th inst. Born in Alexandria, Va., and inheriting the noble qualities which especially distinguish the descendants of the cavaliers, his whole life has been marked by correct dealing. In partnership with the late Isaac Franklin, whose neice (sic) he married, he accumulated a large fortune by his enterprise, energy, pluck, industry and foresight. Retiring several years since from business, he settled upon a handsome farm in Sumner county, and devoted to its improvement and development a liberal expenditure of his means. Those improvements were as solid and as enduring as his own character, and marked hi as a man of far-reaching sagacity and sound common sense. He afterwards in the 1855, bought a handsome property at Beersheba, and the methods which he adopted to make it a permanent and pleasant summer watering place, and the success with which he met showed unmistakably his unerring judgment in all matters of business. He gave to all persons applying therefor (sic) a building lot on the property, with the privilege of using firewood and water from the main tract forever. In this manner Beersheba became the summer homes of some of the most cultivated and eminent gentlemen of the South. Among others were Bishop Polk, Bishop Otey and Col. Dahlgren. Under this wise and liberal policy more than twenty cottages were erected and were occupied ever (sic) summer before the war by their owners and families. The excellence of the society, the purity of the mountain air and the healthfulness of the water, as Gen. Armfield foresaw, attracted hundreds of person every year from every State in the South. The hotel proved a success. In making it so, Gen. Armfield expended more than one hundred thousand dollars. His fondness for Southern society, more than a desire to increase his already large fortune, first led him to this great work, and his name will forever illuminate and illustrate the annals of Beersheba.

As a benevolent man, he had but few equals. Not only for his own family did he expend his means liberally, but the poor and destitute found in hi a firm and steadfast friend. No other passport than honesty and integrity of character was necessary to secure his aid. Destitute of these, though occupying a prominent place in society and the State, no applicant could receive favor at his hands.

He educated by his means more than forty poor children, employing a teacher and giving to his wife the sole control of the school. He never stinted the project, but his only desire and aim was to make it efficient and promotive of the ends for which it was established. The poor mountaineers we know will reverence his memory forever, for we have never seen more respect, admiration and love shown to any one, us (sic) these persons displayed for Gen. Armfield. The writer hereof remembers to have enjoyed Gen. Armfield's hospitality on one occasion, and during a ride to view the magnificent mountain scenery, he was greeted at every house as a friend. Even the poor negroes looked upon him as their fastest friend, and he took delight in bearing with their many infirmities and teaching them the necessity of labor. Of all those owned by him at Beersheba not one left him.

His home at Beersheba was open to all visitors. Seldom will a visitor be found, whose stay at the springs was but for a few days that did not partake of his hospitalities. He regarded Beersheba with pride as his own venture, and in no way could a more direct avenue to his regards be found than in speaking favorably of those celebrated springs. With a strong, industrious intellect and quick apprehension of men, he exercised a prominent influence on all around him. Aided by his accomplished wife, he made his home the abode of all the social virtues.

Some two years ago he was attacked with pneumonia, from which he barely escaped with his life. The attack affected, to some extent, his lungs. A second attack aggravated still more the symptoms. He spent last winter in Florida, thinking it probably that a winter spent there might give him relief. This relief proved to be only temporary. His own mountain air he thought would restore if he could be restored, and accordingly he came back to Beersheba and enjoyed during the hot months of summer a respite from the more acute symptoms of his disease. On the approach of cool weather, however, he relapsed and passed quietly away in the bosom of his family, more than seventy years of age, leaving his many friends to mourn for the death of one so strong in character and so resolute in good.

Legacy: An essay on slavery by the editor

(This is a follow-up of the John Armfield eulogy from pages 139-140.)

In one of my earlier drafts of the Introduction, in an attempt to paint a contrast with their ancestors, I had included the statement, "Six years now since the Civil War ended, Edward and Nannie were, in comparison to their forebears, relatively innocent with regard to slavery." One of my Franklin cousins, Lyn Franklin Hoyt, upon proofreading made the comment to me, "There were no innocents."

After some debate I removed my sentence. Edward and Nannie being so young before the war were never the legal "masters" over other human beings; nevertheless they were children who benefited from the labor of slaves who lived around them and in their homes. Some, like Matilda who is mentioned in the letters, remained with their families after freedom. Was there genuine love and respect among some servants and their former masters? Certainly so, but there was also gross inequality that would continue for generations.

The September 24, 1871 article included in the previous section from the *Nashville Union and American* requires a response. Like the other articles, it was relevant to the story, which was why I included it. Yet I cannot in good conscious end a section of this book with a reference which describes John Armfield as "one so strong in character and so resolute in good," without a follow up.

The man was a slave trader, one of the biggest of the time. It is disturbing for the modern reader, black or white, to read the eulogy author's praise, "In partnership with the late Isaac Franklin, whose neice (sic) he married, he accumulated a large fortune by his enterprise, energy, pluck, industry and foresight." How can one, by the late 1800s, summarize involvement in the American slave trade as "pluck?" Technically, yes, Franklin and Armfield took advantage of the economic situation of the 1830s. Yet it is chilling to ignore the human cost, which is precisely what the eulogy author did. No doubt Armfield did many good things after he exited 'the business.' He was generous in his support of some decent causes and perhaps was a loving family man. But his generosity, and even his support of the family, was supplied by a tainted fortune. I think it a mistake to 'poo-

poo' the fact as an irrelevancy and to believe Armfield 'simply a man of his time.' Nor should it be argued his later generosity totally 'made up' for his former employ. It is not likely that anything he ever did afterwards benefited the thousands of slaves he sent to the hard-labor cotton fields of the Deep South, or their families, which he was directly responsible for tearing apart. He did nothing that remotely mitigated their immeasurable pain.

Edward, our otherwise thoughtful, good-hearted doctor, benefited as Armfield's surrogate son. Similarly there was Nannie's father, Daniel Hillman, who achieved an unhappy superlative by having more slaves working for him than any other individual in the state of Kentucky.

I believe there were consequences, both moral and tangible, of their slave ownership and of the wealth they derived from it. If we take Nannie's father as an example, the later 1870s proved difficult for his iron business as labor costs escalated. A man who at one time was one of the richest in the South, he had much influence and industrial might. Yet he was dependent upon cheap labor. As he deteriorated in the late 1870s he wrote letters to Nannie expressing fears of bankruptcy. He finally succumbed to "melancholia" and died of "exhaustion" at the Kentucky Insane Asylum in 1885. I am sure there were many reasons behind his mental fall, but I believe one of them was the inability to cope with new realities. The Iron King's kingdom had crumbled.

Despite long-term illness, John Armfield himself died peacefully, but again, there were consequences for his heirs. Recall the lawsuit between Edward and his father, John Washington Franklin. Edward's brother, John Armfield Franklin (even the eponym seems a foreshadowing), wanted Edward to have his share of their Uncle John Armfield's estate. Of course what 'estate' are we talking about here? This was slave money, as I have noted—a fortune derived out of the sale of humans and of subsequent business transactions dependent upon it, though admittedly much smaller by this time due to debts and wartime losses. Edward had already received his own share, and now he was pushing for more of it. Did my great-great grandfather ever really consider its ultimate source?

Not all contemporary newspaper writers played the ignorant. In describing the *Franklin v. Franklin* case in *The Examiner* of Gallatin in 1887, this is how the observer concluded his report:

> *The Examiner regrets the necessity of a report of family disagreements even when they get into courts for adjudication, and which is increased by our knowledge of the high standing of the parties and their relation in blood. But it is one of those 'causes celebre' which make their records and cannot be omitted by the faithful journalist.* **It naturally grows out of the distribution of accumulated wealth which originated out of the old regime of slave days when cotton was king in the south and the heirs have inherited its consequences.** (Editor's emphasis.) *And even now other courts are in the process of deciding rights of the heirs of the old Franklin Louisiana and Sumner county property and the will of the mistress of Fairview*[120] *is now in the hands of the lawyers at Nashville. The grandchildren of the old planter, Isaac Franklin, whose slaves in great gangs often passed through Gallatin on their way to the cotton fields of Louisiana, may be in their graves before all of their rights are determined. Fairview still stands in our midst. Its owners have all crossed the river. Its glories as a famous country farm, when the young folks danced and frolicked and made love, have passed away, and they even are now grandfathers and grandmothers or have been laid away to their final rest; its broad acres are green with blue grass where sport blooded horses under the eye of the turfman Charles Reed,*[121] *and costly stables dot its ground where racing men congregate. Such is life.*[122]

These people knew they were privileged and that their wealth was tainted. "There were no innocents." I do think in part they paid the consequences. The Franklin family suffered estrangement and separation because of that lawsuit. John Armfield's own widow, Martha, died broke, relying on the care of relatives, as the amount she inherited was not enough to sustain her. *The Examiner* reporter had some of his facts wrong, for old Isaac Franklin had no children who

---

[120] This is referring to Isaac Franklin's wife, Adelicia. Fairvue plantation is often spelled 'Fairview'.
[121] Charles Reed was a post-war owner of Fairvue plantation, a breeder of race horses. The series of small brick barns as one approaches Fairvue today are individual breed mare stables from Reed's period of ownership.
[122] The complete article is in Appendix 1 on pages 115-117.

survived and therefore no grandchildren—at least not by Adelicia his wife. But I don't think even the otherwise enlightened journalist was referencing Isaac's son, and possible descendants thereby, of the female slave, Lucindy, mother and son whom he sold north to Louisville, before ever Adelicia came to live with him at Fairvue.

We mustn't dwell upon a heavy past, but not to acknowledge it and actively question it is a refusal to move forward with any sense of enlightenment. It was not so very long ago, and the choices our ancestors made still influence current society. Certain voices in modern politics are trying desperately to dismiss the American slave past altogether without ever having properly come to grips with it. For them, the progress made during the Civil Rights Era was sufficient—case closed. For my own part I don't think so at all, nor do I think the Civil Rights Era is over. Far from it.

Ultimately, the point of these 'old letters', 'old pictures', 'old newspapers' is that we, white, black, Native American and others—all part of the American story—learn and grow. We must strive to make the world better, for all, or really there is no point. Edward's twenty-seven letters to Nannie, the pictures and articles I have chosen to go with them, and the story I have woven around these families, I hope will help us all—at least a little—continue to grow.

Acknowledgements

Some time ago, Dr. Joshua Rothman, chair of the history department at the University of Alabama, contacted me wanting to know whether I had any primary source materials on Isaac Franklin or John Armfield. I knew of the existence of Edward's letters (in great cardboard boxes at my parents' house) but had not read them. At first I told him I did not, but eventually I came across the letter that recorded Armfield's death and copied it for Dr. Rothman's use. In time I read and organized all the letters, and found that Armfield is mentioned several times. I concluded the letters should be published, and with all the photographs and materials in my collection to help tell the story, it turned into something bigger, and very quickly. Background on the families was needed, and an afterword, too, so the reader would know what became of Edward and Nannie. Explaining to my Franklin cousin, Kenneth Thomson, Sumner County Historian and President of the Sumner County Historical Society, what I was doing, he promptly located additional photographs in his own collection. He located that key *Examiner* article on 1871 Beersheba which helped enormously in the subsequent identification of many of the people Edward talked about in his letters. To Kenneth I am most grateful.

Other Hillman and Franklin cousins and spouses were also helpful, reading drafts, making suggestions, corroborating on facts, or from whom I borrowed more photos. Along with Kenneth were Lyn Franklin Hoyt, Cherie Breffeihl, Grace Paine Terzian, Sandra Galbraith Long, Sara Franklin Homer, Tom Borcher, Genie Borcher Riddle, Tom Whitney, Jeff Gray, Bob Claxton, Joe Claxton, Ursula Sheffield-Bradshaw, and noted author Judith Hillman Paterson. My parents, Noel and Patsy Martin, read drafts and offered support and helpful reminiscences and resources. My uncle, Tom Martin, provided a number of photos and collected resources.

Some years ago upon request to Land Between the Lakes National Recreation Area, I received in the mail a stack of materials on Daniel Hillman's operations, and I thank Cindy Earls, their Special Events Coordinator.

Suggestions came from the Beersheba Springs Historical Society, and to them I am grateful for their enthusiasm and assistance, particularly Susan Snow, John Adams, and Clopper Almon. They reminded me the value of the letters as Beersheba Springs history, and my desire to footnote the individuals Edward mentions and to include relevant 1871 newspaper articles on Beersheba reflects that. An owner of the old Armfield house, Peg Williams, and her husband Harry, graciously allowed my family to visit the home where Edward wrote most of the letters.

To my own family I express thanks, particularly my father, Noel (named for Edward Noel Franklin), who presented to me a year ago "all that family history stuff" in the two huge cardboard boxes. I am also grateful to my wife, Laura, who helped in the editing process and much encouragement and also patience (I can get obsessive with this sort of thing). I am also grateful to my two sons, Luke and Drew, who occasionally allow me to drag them around on these family history quests to cemeteries and historic sites, for they provide the best company and a captive audience for my tales.

Additional thanks are in order for the following: Michael Ponce of Ponce Law, Mark Brown and Danielle Ullrich of Belmont Mansion, artist Cass Holly, Aaron Thomas of Phone Zone, graphic designer Susan Hofsass Sneed, Kevin Hogan of Spring Haven Mansion, Teresa Bowman and David Mayfield of Historic Rugby, Dr. Benita Howell (retired) and Dr. William Hardwig from the University of Tennessee, Rodney Williams of Vancouver, Washington, Betsy Phillips of the Nashville Scene, Wynnewood State Historic Site, Historic Sam Davis Home and Plantation, Sumner County Museum, and the staffs at the Sumner County Archives and the Tennessee State Library and Archives.

Sources

(Arranged alphabetically by subject matter.)
Anderson Family:

Anderson, Grace Adele—Age 95. Died May 12, 2003 (obituary), The Tennessean, Nashville, Tenn. May 13, 2003, p. 15.

Florida F. Anderson, Find A Grave entry. Accessed 20 February 2018. Memorial no. 128867122, citing Gallatin City Cemetery, Gallatin, Sumner County, Tennessee, USA. Maintained by BBrown (contributor 48207514): *https://www.findagrave.com/memorial/128867122/florida-f-anderson*

Hillman Family Bible, property of Thomas D. Martin, Gallatin, Tenn. The information from this Bible can also be found online at the following link: *http://home.rootsweb.com/~tnsumner/brhillman.htm* and also at the Tennessee State Library and Archives in the Hillman surname file.

Hillman Family—Haddonfield, N.J., Branch—Genealogy, 1932, no author credited, 1932. "Reference CS, 71, .H654, 1932" located at the Tennessee State Library and Archives. 31-page manuscript contains great detail on the genealogy of this branch of the Hillman family.

Walter Leake Anderson, Find A Grave entry. Accessed 20 February 2018. Memorial no. 128868538, citing Gallatin City Cemetery, Gallatin, Sumner County, Tennessee, USA. Maintained by BBrown (contributor 48207514): *https://www.findagrave.com/memorial/128868538/walter-leake-anderson*

Archer Family (Stevenson Archer and Jane Cage "Blanche" Franklin Archer):

Blanche Franklin Archer, Find A Grave Entry. Accessed 20 February 2018. Memorial no. 129800983, citing Churchville Presbyterian Church Cemetery, Churchville, Harford County, Maryland, USA; Maintained by PAC (contributor 46915292): *https://www.findagrave.com/memorial/129800983/blanche-archer*

John Armfield of Beersheba Springs, Isabel Howell. 2011 reprint. Beersheba Springs Historical Society. Page 47. The original articles by Howell appeared in the Tennessee Historical Quarterly in 1943 and 1944.

Stevenson Archer: Defaulted Defalcation, entry by Dirk Langefeld, 2009, in The Downfall Dictionary: *http://downfalldictionary.blogspot.com/2009/06/stevenson-archer-defaulted-defalcation.html*

Stevenson Archer, Find A Grave Entry. Accessed 20 February 2018. Memorial no. 7844491, citing Churchville Presbyterian Church Cemetery, Churchville, Harford County, Maryland, USA; Maintained by Find A Grave: *https://www.findagrave.com/memorial/7844491/stevenson-archer*

Van Bibber family scrapbook, put together by Armfield Franklin Van Bibber (a son of Edward's sister, Adele Franklin Van Bibber), in the possession of descendant W. T. (Tom) Whitney of South Paris, Maine. Certain information on the Archers and the Van Bibbers came from this.

Armfield Family (John Armfield and Martha Franklin Armfield):

"DNA Evidence for Direct Descendancy of Rodney Williams from John Armfield," unpublished document compiled and provided by Rodney Williams, Vancouver, Washington. 2018.

Gen. John Armfield, Nashville Union and American Nashville, Tenn., Sunday, September 24, 1871.

John Armfield of Beersheba Springs, by Isabel Howell. 2011 reprint. Beersheba Springs Historical Society. The original articles appeared in the Tennessee Historical Quarterly in 1943 and 1944.

John Armfield portrait on page 95 is from a print located at the Tennessee State Library and Archives. It is labeled in italics following: "*Isaac Franklin (1789-1846). [This may be misidentified. Possibly a portrait of John Armfield, Franklin's slave trading partner].*" Nell Savage Mahoney Papers, Accession # THS 457, THS 681, File location: THS VI-B-7, Box 33, Folder 46. Photo--Collins-Cooley. Artist--Washington B. Cooper. It can also be found on this web page: *http://tnsos.org/tsla/imagesearch/citation.php?ImageID=29818* (Based on evidence given in conversation in 2017 between the editor and Franklin family descendant and Sumner County official Historian, Kenneth Thomson, Martin is confident the image is of John Armfield. Thomson was able to describe confidently the history of the image based on long-ago conversations with earlier Franklin family owners of the original painting whom he knew personally. In addition, the image was for a time being used by Belmont Mansion in their brochure as Isaac Franklin, and Thomson also convinced them that the image is actually John Armfield, prompting Belmont to stop labeling the image as Franklin. Consider also that if Washington B. Cooper was the artist as attributed, there is a painting already of Isaac Franklin by him—also used in this book—and the two subjects are clearly different men. The evidence weighs in favor of its identity being John Armfield.)

John Armfield, Wikipedia. *https://en.wikipedia.org/wiki/John_Armfield*

Martha R. Franklin Armfield, Find A Grave entry. Accessed 19 February 2018, Memorial no. 80034117, citing Gallatin City Cemetery, Gallatin, Sumner County, Tennessee, USA; Maintained by OBXr (contributor 46634091): *https://www.findagrave.com/memorial/80034117/martha-r.-armfield*

Retracing Slavery's Trail of Tears, by Edward Ball. Smithsonian, November 2015.

Spring Haven Mansion (Hendersonville), official website: *http://www.springhavenmansion.com/*

See also mentions in newspaper articles in Appendix 2.

Baber Family:

Sarah Frances Baber Franklin, Find A Grave entry. Accessed 20 February 2018. Memorial no. 88950988, citing Gallatin City Cemetery, Gallatin, Sumner County, Tennessee, USA. Maintained by OBXr (contributor 46634091): *https://www.findagrave.com/memorial/88950988/sarah-frances-franklin*

Foxland Southern Grill, Foxland Harbor Golf and Country Club webpage: *http://www.foxlandharbor.com/foxland-southern-grill/*

Foxland Southern Grill, Hidden Gem of Sumner Dining Scene, by Jennifer Easton. July 8, 2016, updated July 12, 2016. Tennessean website: *https://www.tennessean.com/story/news/local/sumner/gallatin/2016/07/08/foxland-southern-grill-offers-tasteful-experience/86795694/*

Banks, A. D.:

Major A. D. Banks (death notice), The Baltimore Sun, July 23, 1881 page 4: *https://www.newspapers.com/newspage/214419691/*

Major A. D. Banks, bio mention on page 392 of After the war: A Southern Tour, May 1, 1865 to May 1, 1866, by Whitelaw Reid, originally published London: Sampson Low, et.al. 1866. Full text here: *https://quod.lib.umich.edu/m/moa/AFJ8942.0001.001?rgn=main;view=fulltext*

See also mentions in newspaper articles in Appendix 2.

Barbour Family (Caldwell "Kit" Barbour and Mary Ann Hillman Barbour):

Dr. Caldwell "Kit" Barbour, Find A Grave entry. Accessed 20 February 2018. Memorial no. 123804401, citing East End Cemetery, Cadiz, Trigg County, Kentucky, USA; Maintained by Brandy Wells Murray (contributor 4722656): *https://www.findagrave.com/memorial/123804401/caldwell-barbour*

Mary Ann Hillman Barbour, Find A Grave entry. Accessed 20 February 2018. Memorial no. 123804632, citing East End Cemetery, Cadiz, Trigg County, Kentucky, USA; Maintained by Brandy Wells Murray (contributor 4722656): *https://www.findagrave.com/memorial/123804632*

Bass, John Meredith:

Beersheba Springs, a History: Volume II. Families, Homes, Lore, and More, edited by Clopper Almon. 2010. Beersheba Springs Historical Society. Page 17.

Bate, William B.:

William B. Bate, Wikipedia. *https://en.wikipedia.org/wiki/William_B._Bate*

Beersheba Springs, Tennessee:

Beersheba Springs, a History: Volume I. General History, the Hotel-Assembly, and Shops, edited by Clopper Almon. 2010. Beersheba Springs Historical Society.

Beersheba Springs, a History: Volume II. Families, Homes, Lore, and More, edited by Clopper Almon. 2010. Beersheba Springs Historical Society.

Beersheba Springs, a History: Volume III. Classics, edited by Clopper Almon, 2011. Beersheba Springs Historical Society.

The Beersheba Springs Diaries of L. Virginia French, edited by Herschel Gower. Beersheba Springs Historical Society. 1986.

Beersheba Springs The Columbia Herald. Columbia, Tenn., July 28, 1871

Beersheba Springs, The Examiner. Gallatin, Tenn., Saturday, August 19, 1871.

Beersheba Springs, Grundy County, Tenn. (advertisement), Nashville Union and American, Nashville, Tenn., Saturday, May 13, 1871.

The Grand Bal Masque Last Thursday Night, Republican Banner, Nashville, Tenn., August 13, 1871.

John Armfield of Beersheba Springs, by Isabel Howell. 2011 reprint. Beersheba Springs Historical Society. The original articles appeared in the Tennessee Historical Quarterly in 1943 and 1944.

The Mask Ball a Grand and Brilliant Affair, Nashville Union and American, Tuesday, August 15, 1871. *http://chroniclingamerica.loc.gov/lccn/sn85033699/1871-08-15/ed-1/*

Borcher Family (Charles Allen Borcher and Florida Noel Franklin Borcher):

Charles Allen Borcher, Memorial page. Memorial Networks web page sponsored by Laughlin Service Funeral Home of Huntsville, AL: *http://www.laughlinservice.com/memsol.cgi?user_id=840780*

Florida Noel Franklin Borcher, Memorial page. Memorial Networks web page sponsored by Laughlin Service Funeral Home of Huntsville, AL:
http://www.laughlinservice.com/memsol.cgi?user_id=1975607

Hillman Family Bible, property of Thomas D. Martin, Gallatin, Tenn. The information from this Bible can also be found online at the following link: http://home.rootsweb.com/~tnsumner/brhillman.htm and also at the Tennessee State Library and Archives in the Hillman surname file.

Hillman Family—Haddonfield, N.J., Branch—Genealogy, 1932, no author credited, 1932. "Reference CS, 71, .H654, 1932" located at the Tennessee State Library and Archives. 31-page manuscript contains great detail on the genealogy of this branch of the Hillman family.

Buford, Lizinka Elliston:

Lizinka Elliston Buford, Find A Grave entry. Accessed 20 February 2018. Memorial no. 12876083, citing Mount Olivet Cemetery, Nashville, Davidson County, Tennessee, Maintained by Tennessee Irish (contributor 46623970): https://www.findagrave.com/cgi-bin/fg.cgi?page=gr&GSln=Buford&GSfn=Lizinka&GSbyrel=all&GSdyrel=all&GSob=n&GRid=12876083&df=all&

Clark, Richard:

Beersheba Springs, a History: Volume I. General History, the Hotel-Assembly, and Shops, edited by Clopper Almon. 2010. Beersheba Springs Historical Society. Page 21.

John Armfield of Beersheba Springs, Isabel Howell. 2011 reprint. Beersheba Springs Historical Society. Pp. 87-88.

Craighead Family (James Brown Craighead and Alethea Allison Craighead):

Biography of James Brown Craighead, originally from Biographical and Historical Memoirs of Eastern Arkansas. Chicago: Goodspeed Publishers, 1890:
http://files.usgwarchives.net/ar/mississippi/bios/craigheadjb.txt

Eve, Paul Fitzsimmons:

Dr. Paul Fitzsimmons Eve, bio, The Academy of Richmond County web page:
https://sites.google.com/site/thearchalloffame/home/2014-15-recipients/dr-paul-fitzsimmons-eve

Ewin Family (William G. Ewin and Martha Jane "Mattie" Hillman Ewin):

Ancestral Chronological Record of the Hillman Family—1550-1905, by Harry W. Hillman 1905, out of print full text appears here:
https://archive.org/stream/ancestralchronol00lchill/ancestralchronol00lchill_djvu.txt

Civil War Days and Those Surnames, website (Capt. William G. Ewin):
http://civilwarthosesurnames.blogspot.com/search?q=Ewin

The Diary of Nannie Haskins Williams: A Southern Woman's Story of Rebellion and Reconstruction, 1863-1890, edited by Minoa D. Uffelman, Ellen Kanervo, Phyllis Smith, and Eleanor Williams. University of Tennessee Press, 2014. Pages 13-14, 50. Consult its index for more references to Mattie Hillman.

The Family History Collection of Bob Claxton, Franklin, Tennessee. Bob is one of the few descendants of Capt. William G. and Martha Jane "Mattie" Hillman Ewin. His collection contains many personal and expense journals from George Washington Hillman, Capt. William G. Ewin, and Mattie Hillman Ewin.

Hillman Family—Haddonfield, N.J., Branch—Genealogy, 1932, no author credited, 1932. "Reference CS, 71, .H654, 1932" located at the Tennessee State Library and Archives. 31-page manuscript contains great detail on the genealogy of this branch of the Hillman family.

Waverly Church of Christ (Mattie Ewin as a founder), official website: *http://www.waverlychurchofchrist.org/about.html*

Ewing, Robert:

Nashville City Directory for the years 1872, 1873, 1874, 1875, 1876, 1877, 1878, and 1879.

See also mentions in newspaper articles in Appendix 2.

Franklin, Charles "Charlie" Hillman (and Alexandrine "Didine" Groslevin Franklin):

Alexandrine G. Franklin, Find A Grave entry. Accessed 20 February 2018. Memorial no. 109170264, citing Greenwood Cemetery, Eustis, Lake County, Florida, USA. Maintained by Tom & Gloria Smith (contributor 47538594): *https://www.findagrave.com/memorial/109170264*

Charles Hillman Franklin, Billion Graves website entry. *https://billiongraves.com/grave/Charles-Hillman-Franklin/10111718*

Hillman Family Bible, property of Thomas D. Martin, Gallatin, Tenn. The information from this Bible can also be found online at the following link: *http://home.rootsweb.com/~tnsumner/brhillman.htm* and also at the Tennessee State Library and Archives in the Hillman surname file.

Hillman Family—Haddonfield, N.J., Branch—Genealogy, 1932, no author credited, 1932. "Reference CS, 71, .H654, 1932" located at the Tennessee State Library and Archives. 31-page manuscript contains great detail on the genealogy of this branch of the Hillman family.

The Tennessean, (wedding of Charlie Franklin and Maud McAlister), Nashville, Sunday, January 13, 1907, p. 15.

Franklin, Daniel Hillman "Hillman":

D. Hillman Franklin, Died of Morphine Poisoning at Memphis Last Night, The Nashville American, Nashville, Oct. 14, 1904, page 3.

Hillman Family Bible, property of Thomas D. Martin, Gallatin, Tenn. The information from this Bible can also be found online at the following link: *http://home.rootsweb.com/~tnsumner/brhillman.htm* and also at the Tennessee State Library and Archives in the Hillman surname file.

Hillman Family—Haddonfield, N.J., Branch—Genealogy, 1932, no author credited, 1932. "Reference CS, 71, .H654, 1932" located at the Tennessee State Library and Archives. 31-page manuscript contains great detail on the genealogy of this branch of the Hillman family.

Hillman Franklin, His Death in a Hospital in Memphis Thursday Night, The Tennessean, Nashville, Saturday, October 15, 1904.

Franklin, Edward Noel:

Confederate Veteran (Edward's ad for drug cure), May, 1903. Page 237: https://archive.org/stream/confederateveter11conf#page/237/mode/1up

Dr. Edward Nolen Franklin, Find A Grave entry. (Ed. note: Edward's middle name was Noel, not 'Nolen'. The mistake is sometimes found elsewhere.) Accessed 20 February 2018. Memorial no. 91540629, citing Mount Olivet Cemetery, Nashville, Davidson County, Tennessee, USA. Maintained by Jerry G. Marable (contributor 46969784): https://www.findagrave.com/memorial/91540629/edward-nolen-franklin

The Family History Collection of Terry Martin, Gallatin, Tennessee. For use in the current volume, aside from many vintage photographs, letters and letterheads, invitations and lists, there are included a number of saved obituaries from vintage papers, financial records, receipts, letters from various Hillman relatives, volumes of Nannie's music from school, and other Hillman and Franklin items, saved by Nannie Hillman Franklin, passed down through the family to Martin.

The Family History Collection of Thomas D. Martin, Gallatin, Tennessee. For use in the current volume were a number of key photographs, in addition to Edward and Nannie's expense journal.

The Goodspeed Histories of Sumner, Smith, Macon, Trousdale, Counties of Tennessee, reprinted from Goodspeed's History of Tennessee, originally published 1887. Published by Woodward & Stinson Printing Co. (The photocopied pages used by the editor containing biographical sketches of Dr. John W. Franklin and of Ed N. Franklin, M.D., contain many side notes and old errors corrected by Sumner County Historian, Kenneth Thomson.)

The Historical Collection of Kenneth C. Thomson, Jr., Gallatin, Tennessee. For use in this volume, aside from many vintage photographs, there are included a number of photocopied articles and obituaries from old newspapers relating to the Franklins, on the lawsuit between Edward Noel Franklin and John Washington Franklin, some biographical sketches photocopied from older local history publications from the 1800s and early 1900s. Some of this material can also be found at the Sumner County Archives.

Nashville City Directory for the years 1872, 1873, 1874, 1875, 1876, 1877, 1878, and 1879.

Nashville Union and American, Friday, January 5, 1872 (Edward and Nannie marriage announcement). http://chroniclingamerica.loc.gov/lccn/sn85033699/1872-01-05/ed-1/seq-4/

Nashville Union and American, Saturday, January 6, 1872 (Edward and Nannie marriage license issued). http://chroniclingamerica.loc.gov/lccn/sn85033699/1872-01-06/ed-1/seq-3/

See also the newspaper articles in Appendix 1 and 2.

Franklin, Isaac (and Adelicia Hayes Franklin Acklen Cheatham):

Belmont Mansion, official website: http://www.belmontmansion.com/history

The Half Has Never Been Told: Slavery and The Making of American Capitalism, by Edward E. Baptist, Basic Books, New York, 2014. Chapter 7, "Seed." Pages 233-234 (Isaac Franklin's slave Girl, Lucindy.)

Isaac Franklin, Slave Trader and Planter of the Old South, by Wendell Holmes Stephenson. 1968 reprint edition by Peter Smith. Originally published 1938 by Louisiana State University Press.

Isaac Franklin, Wikipedia. https://en.wikipedia.org/wiki/Isaac_Franklin

Isaac Franklin Plantation, Wikipedia. https://en.wikipedia.org/wiki/Isaac_Franklin_Plantation

The Man We'd Love to Forget: Isaac Franklin's Money Had a Major Influence on Modern Day Nashville—Despite the Blood in It. Article by Betsy Phillips, May 7, 2015, for the Nashville Scene: http://www.nashvillescene.com/news/pith-in-the-wind/article/13059116/isaac-franklins-money-had-a-major-influence-on-modernday-nashville-despite-the-blood-on-it

Masters of the Big House: Elite Slaveholders of the Mid-Nineteenth Century South, by William Koffman Scarborough. Louisiana State University Press. 2003. (Daniel Hillman slave ownership, page 462. Isaac Franklin slave ownership, pages 124, 125, 430, 454.)

Retracing Slavery's Trail of Tears, by Edward Ball. Smithsonian, November 2015.

The Saga of Fairvue 1832-1977, by Margaret Lindley Warden. Published by Warden. 1977.

Franklin, James (and Mary Lauderdale Franklin):

Grave Marking Ceremony Held for Cpl. James Franklin, Hendersonville Standard website article, November 4, 2016. http://hendersonvillestandard.com/grave-marking-ceremony-held-for-cpl-james-franklin-cms-10499

The Historic Blue Grass Line, published by the Nashville-Gallatin Interurban Railway, Nashville, Tennessee. 1913.

Old Sumner: A History of Sumner County Tennessee from 1805-1861, by Walter T. Durham. Sumner County Library Board. 1972.

Passing on the Torch for a Golden Era, Your Williamson.com: http://www.yourwilliamson.com/passing-torch-golden-era/

Right of Preemption: http://www.cumberlandpioneers.com/preemptions.html

Save Captain James Franklin's Grave, website (ed. note. It is now understood that he was a corporal, not a captain. As of 2018, the website author has not yet made a change to the website's main title.): http://savejamesfranklinsgrave.blogspot.com/p/who-is-james-franklin-sumner-county.html

William Lee Golden, (See section on "The Golden Era Plantation") Wikipedia: https://en.wikipedia.org/wiki/William_Lee_Golden

Franklin, John Armfield:

Civil War Diary Fragments of John Armfield Franklin, 1864-1865, unpublished manuscript. Copy belonging to Lyn Franklin Hoyt given her by Cherie Beffeihl.

Death of Armfield Franklin, The Columbia Herald, Columbia, Tennessee. Nov. 24, 1871.

See also the newspaper articles in Appendix 1.

Franklin, John Washington: (For 1st wife, Florida Mercer Noel Franklin, see 'Noel Family.' For 2nd wife, Sarah Baber Franklin, see 'Baber Family.')

Dr. John W. Franklin House "Oakley," National Register of Historic Places, Inventory-Nomination Form: https://npgallery.nps.gov/GetAsset/0503f88d-e63a-4b50-a0c6-0ea4656f1435

Franklin Family Bible, property of Robert Orr Franklin, photocopied pages in possession of Lyn Franklin Hoyt, Nashville, Tennessee.

Franklin surname file, Sumner County Archives.

The Goodspeed Histories of Sumner, Smith, Macon, Trousdale, Counties of Tennessee, reprinted from Goodspeed's History of Tennessee, originally published 1887. Published by Woodward & Stinson Printing Co. (The photocopied pages used by the editor containing biographical sketches of Dr. John W. Franklin and of Ed N. Franklin, M.D., contain many side notes and old errors corrected by Sumner County Historian, Kenneth Thomson.)

The Historical Collection of Kenneth C. Thomson, Jr., Gallatin, Tennessee. For use in this volume, aside from many vintage photographs, there are included a number of photocopied articles and obituaries from old newspapers relating to the Franklins, on the lawsuit between Edward Noel Franklin and John Washington Franklin, some biographical sketches photocopied from older local history publications from the 1800s and early 1900s. Some of this material can also be found at the Sumner County Archives.

The Historic Blue Grass Line, published by the Nashville-Gallatin Interurban Railway, Nashville, Tennessee. 1913.

Nine Tennessee Sites Added to National Register of Historic Places (Trousdale-Baskerville House), article appearing in Clarksville Online website: *http://www.clarksvilleonline.com/2009/09/19/nine-tennessee-sites-added-to-the-national-register-of-historic-places/*

Oakley (Gallatin, Tennessee), Wikipedia. (Ed. note. Though the article claims Strickland as the architect, this is disputed by some.): *https://en.wikipedia.org/wiki/Oakley_(Gallatin,_Tennessee)*

Trousdale Baskerville House, National Register of Historic Places Registration Form: *https://npgallery.nps.gov/GetAsset/91a18706-807e-46a5-8801-526348761233*

Van Bibber family scrapbook, put together by Armfield Franklin Van Bibber (a son of Edward's sister, Adele Franklin Van Bibber), in the possession of descendant W. T. (Tom) Whitney of South Paris, Maine. Certain information on the Archers and the Van Bibbers came from this. Also, a key obituary of John Washington Franklin mentioning how his first wife Florida died is pasted in this.

See also the newspaper articles in Appendix 1.

Franklin, Matilda:

Matilda Franklin (obituary). The Daily American, Nashville, Tennessee. March 3, 1878.

Matilda Franklin portrait. Tennessee State Library and Archives. File location: II-J-4, Folder 13. It can also be found on this web page: *http://tnsos.org/tsla/imagesearch/citation.php?ImageID=32264*

Franklin, Nannie (Ann Fredonia) Hillman:

Ancestral Chronological Record of the Hillman Family—1550-1905, by Harry W. Hillman 1905, out of print full text appears here:
https://archive.org/stream/ancestralchronol00lchill/ancestralchronol00lchill_djvu.txt

Ann Fredonia "Nannie" Hillman Franklin, Find A Grave entry. Accessed 20 February 2018. Memorial no. 91540372, citing Mount Olivet Cemetery, Nashville, Davidson County, Tennessee, USA. Maintained by Jerry G. Marable (contributor 46969784):
https://www.findagrave.com/memorial/91540372/ann-fredonia-franklin

The Diary of Nannie Haskins Williams: A Southern Woman's Story of Rebellion and Reconstruction, 1863-1890, edited by Minoa D. Uffelman, Ellen Kanervo, Phyllis Smith, and Eleanor Williams. University of Tennessee Press, 2014. Pages 13-14, 50. See its index for additional references to Nannie, who is referred to by the diary author as "Annie" Hillman.

The Family History Collection of Terry Martin, Gallatin, Tennessee. For use in the current volume, aside from many vintage photographs, letters and letterheads, invitations and lists, there are included a number of saved obituaries from vintage papers, financial records, receipts, letters from various Hillman relatives, volumes of Nannie's music from school, and other Hillman and Franklin items, saved by Nannie Hillman Franklin, passed down through the family to Martin.

The Family History Collection of Thomas D. Martin, Gallatin, Tennessee. For use in the current volume were a number of key photographs, in addition to Edward and Nannie's expense journal.

Hillman Family—Haddonfield, N.J., Branch—Genealogy, 1932, no author credited, 1932. "Reference CS, 71, .H654, 1932" located at the Tennessee State Library and Archives. 31-page manuscript contains great detail on the genealogy of this branch of the Hillman family.

The Historical Collection of Kenneth C. Thomson, Jr., Gallatin, Tennessee. For use in this volume, aside from many vintage photographs, there are included a number of photocopied articles and obituaries from old newspapers relating to the Franklins, on the lawsuit between Edward Noel Franklin and John Washington Franklin, some biographical sketches photocopied from older local history publications from the 1800s and early 1900s. Some of this material can also be found at the Sumner County Archives.

Tennessee Portrait Projects, website (Ann Fredonia "Nannie" Hillman Franklin):
http://tnportraits.org/franklin-anne-nannie.htm

Thomas Hughes Free Public Library, Rugby, Tennessee. The historic library contains only volumes predating 1900. Two of Nannie Hillman Franklin's French books were donated in the past to the library. Also noted for the purposes of the research are the many volumes on Phrenology.

Franklin, Smith Claiborne (and Elizabeth Alcorn Cage Franklin):

Elizabeth Alcorn Cage Franklin, Find A Grave entry. Accessed 19 February 2018, Memorial no. 97997894, citing Gallatin City Cemetery, Gallatin, Sumner County, Tennessee, USA; Maintained by Catherine Clemens Sevenau (contributor 47082189): *https://www.findagrave.com/cgi-bin/fg.cgi?page=gr&GRid=97997894*

Smith Claiborne Franklin, Find A Grave entry. Accessed 20 February 2018, Memorial no. 97998042, citing Gallatin City Cemetery, Gallatin, Sumner County, Tennessee, USA; Maintained by Catherine Clemens Sevenau (contributor 47082189): *https://www.findagrave.com/cgi-bin/fg.cgi?page=gr&GRid=97998042*

Franklin v. Franklin:

After a Third Trial a Verdict is Given in Favor of Dr. Ed. N. Franklin, The Examiner, Gallatin, Tennessee, 1887 (uncertain date), photocopy provided by Sumner County Historian, Kenneth Thomson.

Barred by Limitations, The Courier Journal, Louisville, Kentucky, Friday, January 15, 1892, page 2. *http://courier-journal.newspapers.com/image/32440597/*

Celebrated Case: The Court Decides in Setting Up the Will of Armfield Franklin, The Daily American, Nashville, Tennessee, Friday, March 14, 1890, page 6. *https://www.newspapers.com/image/118982117/*

A Celebrated Lawsuit: Contest Over the Will of Armfield Franklin, The Daily American, Nashville, Tennessee, Friday, February 27, 1891, page 2. *https://www.newspapers.com/image/119037226/*

Franklin vs. Franklin: A Celebrated Case on Trial at Gallatin, The Daily American, Nashville, Tennessee, Friday, March 7, 1890, page 1. *https://www.newspapers.com/image/118980888/*

The Franklin Will Case Decided at Gallatin, The Daily American, Nashville, Tennessee, Thursday, November 10, 1887, page 7. *https://www.newspapers.com/image/119314744/*

Franklin vs. Franklin Occupies the Week—Sensational Evidence, The Examiner, Gallatin, Tennessee, 1887 (uncertain date), photocopy provided by Sumner County Historian, Kenneth Thomson.

Reports of Cases Argued and Determined in the Supreme Court of Tennessee, Vol. VII, Nashville, TN 1892. Printed by Marshall & Bruce. The court case of Franklin v Franklin. Pages 119-134. *https://books.google.com/books?id=klcLAAAAYAAJ&pg=PA121&lpg=PA121&dq=%22Franklin+v+Franklin%22+%22John+Armfield%22&source=bl&ots=CrYLuVdbVO&sig=tDPHwuHti1cRlXJFhjZho8-dznM&hl=en&sa=X&ved=0ahUKEwjh9qne35_UAhVE7CYKHWwWDb8Q6AEIKjAB#v=onepage&q=%22Franklin%20v%20Franklin%22%20%22John%20Armfield%22&f=false*

Gallatin and Sumner County, Tennessee:

Commission Creates New County Tourism Board, by Sherry Mitchell, November 3, 2017. Gallatin News website: *https://www.gallatinnews.com/news/government/commission-creates-new-county-tourism-board/article_d836a6ca-c0ad-11e7-8cf3-eb6c326f1840.html*

Dr. John W. Franklin House "Oakley," National Register of Historic Places, Inventory-Nomination Form: *https://npgallery.nps.gov/GetAsset/0503f88d-e63a-4b50-a0c6-0ea4656f1435*

Episcopal Mission Founded in 1881: *http://www.rootsweb.ancestry.com/~tnsumner//chep.htm*

Foxland Southern Grill, Foxland Harbor Golf and Country Club webpage: *http://www.foxlandharbor.com/foxland-southern-grill/*

Foxland Southern Grill, Hidden Gem of Sumner Dining Scene, by Jennifer Easton. July 8, 2016, updated July 12, 2016. Tennessean website: *https://www.tennessean.com/story/news/local/sumner/gallatin/2016/07/08/foxland-southern-grill-offers-tasteful-experience/86795694/*

The Historic Blue Grass Line, published by the Nashville-Gallatin Interurban Railway, Nashville, Tennessee. 1913.

Images of America: Around Gallatin and Sumner County, by Dee Gee Lester and Kenneth Calvin Thomson, Jr. Arcadia Publishing. 1998.

Images of America: Around Gallatin and Sumner County-Volume II, by Dee Gee Lester and Kenneth Calvin Thomson, Jr. Arcadia Publishing. 1998.

Isaac Franklin Plantation, Wikipedia. *https://en.wikipedia.org/wiki/Isaac_Franklin_Plantation*

Nine Tennessee Sites Added to National Register of Historic Places (Trousdale-Baskerville House), article appearing in Clarksville Online website: *http://www.clarksvilleonline.com/2009/09/19/nine-tennessee-sites-added-to-the-national-register-of-historic-places/*

Oakley (Gallatin, Tennessee), Wikipedia. (Ed. note. Though the article claims Strickland as the architect, this is disputed by some.): *https://en.wikipedia.org/wiki/Oakley_(Gallatin,_Tennessee)*

Old Sumner: A History of Sumner County Tennessee from 1805-1861, by Walter T. Durham. Sumner County Library Board. 1972.

Passing on the Torch for a Golden Era, Your Williamson.com: *http://www.yourwilliamson.com/passing-torch-golden-era/*

Spring Haven Mansion (Hendersonville), official website: *http://www.springhavenmansion.com/*

Trousdale Baskerville House, National Register of Historic Places Registration Form: *https://npgallery.nps.gov/GetAsset/91a18706-807e-46a5-8801-526348761233*

William Lee Golden, (See section on "The Golden Era Plantation") Wikipedia: *https://en.wikipedia.org/wiki/William_Lee_Golden*

Gentry Family:

Emily S. Gentry Hillman, Find A Grave entry. Accessed 19 February 2018, Memorial no. 7358921, citing Mount Olivet Cemetery, Nashville, Davidson County, Tennessee, USA; Maintained by Find A Grave (contributor 8): *https://www.findagrave.com/memorial/7358921/emily-s.-hillman*

Gentry Family Bible, property of the editor.

Mary A. Gentry Hillman, Find A Grave entry. Accessed 19 February 2018, Memorial no. 7358926, citing Mount Olivet Cemetery, Nashville, Davidson County, Tennessee, USA; Maintained by Find A Grave (contributor 8): *https://www.findagrave.com/memorial/7358926/mary-a.-hillman*

Meredith Poindexter Gentry, Wikipedia. *https://en.wikipedia.org/wiki/Meredith_Poindexter_Gentry*

Mrs. Mary Gentry Hillman, eulogy article appearing in Confederate Veteran. Volume XVI. Nashville, Tennessee, 1908. Page 292.
https://books.google.com/books?id=ySFEAQAAMAAJ&pg=PA292&dq=Daniel%20Hillman&hl=en&sa=X&ved=0ahUKEwiWo5TOtrjXAhXBZCYKHeP4ANM4ChC7BQhHMAc#v=onepage&q=Daniel%20Hillman&f=false

Goodrich Family (Justus Buck Goodrich and Jane Huston Hillman Goodrich):

Hillman Family—Haddonfield, N.J., Branch—Genealogy, 1932, no author credited, 1932. "Reference CS, 71, .H654, 1932" located at the Tennessee State Library and Archives. 31-page manuscript contains great detail on the genealogy of this branch of the Hillman family.

Jane Hillman Goodrich, Find A Grave entry. Accessed 20 February 2018, Memorial no. 125702505, citing Little River Cemetery, Cadiz, Trigg County, Kentucky, USA. Maintained by Brandy Wells Murray (contributor 47722656): *https://www.findagrave.com/memorial/125702505/jane-goodrich*

Justus Buck Goodrich, Find A Grave entry. Accessed 20 February 2018, Memorial no. 125702513, citing Little River Cemetery, Cadiz, Trigg County, Kentucky, USA. Maintained by Brandy Wells Murray (contributor 47722656): h*ttps://www.findagrave.com/memorial/125702513*

Guild Family:

Josephus Conn Guild, by Walter T. Durham. The Tennessee Encyclopedia of History and Culture, Version 2.0: *http://tennesseeencyclopedia.net/entry.php?rec=580*

Walter J. Guild, Find A Grave entry. Accessed 20 February 2018. Memorial no. 99051280, citing Gallatin City Cemetery, Gallatin, Sumner County, Tennessee, USA. Maintained by OBXr (contributor 46634091): *https://www.findagrave.com/cgi-bin/fg.cgi?page=gr&GRid=99051280*

Hillman, Bellfield Carter:

Ancestral Chronological Record of the Hillman Family—1550-1905, by Harry W. Hillman 1905, out of print full text appears here:
https://archive.org/stream/ancestralchronol00lchill/ancestralchronol00lchill_djvu.txt

Hillman Family—Haddonfield, N.J., Branch—Genealogy, 1932, no author credited, 1932. "Reference CS, 71, .H654, 1932" located at the Tennessee State Library and Archives. 31-page manuscript contains great detail on the genealogy of this branch of the Hillman family.

Nashville Daily American, 1876, A Genealogical Scrapbook, researched and compiled by Jonathan Kennon Thompson Smith, Copyright Jonathan K. T. Smith, 2003 (record of death of B. Carter Hillman): *http://www.tngenweb.org/records/davidson/misc/nda76/nda76-15.htm*

Hillman, Charles Ellis:

Ancestral Chronological Record of the Hillman Family—1550-1905, by Harry W. Hillman 1905, out of print full text appears here:
https://archive.org/stream/ancestralchronol00lchill/ancestralchronol00lchill_djvu.txt

Hillman Family—Haddonfield, N.J., Branch—Genealogy, 1932, no author credited, 1932. "Reference CS, 71, .H654, 1932" located at the Tennessee State Library and Archives. 31-page manuscript contains great detail on the genealogy of this branch of the Hillman family.

Hillman surname file, Tennessee State Library and Archives.

Nashville Union and American, Sunday, October 15, 1871 (Charles E. Hillman listed as a board member on the advertisements for two companies).
http://chroniclingamerica.loc.gov/lccn/sn85033699/1871-10-15/ed-1/seq-4/

Hillman, Daniel (Jr.)—Nannie's father: (For 1st wife, Ann Jones Marable Hillman, see 'Marable Family.' For 2nd wife, Mary Gentry Hillman, see 'Gentry Family.')

Ancestral Chronological Record of the Hillman Family—1550-1905, by Harry W. Hillman 1905, out of print full text appears here:
https://archive.org/stream/ancestralchronol00lchill/ancestralchronol00lchill_djvu.txt

County of Trigg, Kentucky Historical and Biographical, edited by William Henry Perrin, 1884, bio sketch of Daniel Hillman, page 258-259.

Daniel Hannold Hillman, Jr., Find A Grave entry. Accessed 19 February 2018, Memorial no. 7358923, citing Mount Olivet Cemetery, Nashville, Davidson County, Tennessee USA; Maintained by Find A Grave (contributor 8): *https://www.findagrave.com/memorial/7358923*

Early Ironmasters Played Critical Role in Area's Growth, by George Zepp. Article appeared in The Tennessean, Wednesday, March 29, 2006.

Families of Iron: The Hillmans—a timeline prepared by Cindy Earls, Special Events Coordinator, Land Between the Lakes National Recreation Area.

Forts Henry, Heiman, and Donelson: The African American Experience, by Susan Hawkins. This was her master's thesis (circa 2003) presented to the Dept. of History, Murray State University, Murray, KY. *https://www.nps.gov/parkhistory/online_books/fodo/hawkins.pdf*

The Family History Collection of Terry Martin, Gallatin, Tennessee. For use in the current volume, aside from many vintage photographs, letters and letterheads, invitations and lists, there are included a number of saved obituaries from vintage papers, financial records, receipts, letters from various Hillman relatives, volumes of Nannie's music from school, and other Hillman and Franklin items, saved by Nannie Hillman Franklin, passed down through the family to Martin.

Hillman Family—Haddonfield, N.J., Branch—Genealogy, 1932, no author credited, 1932. "Reference CS, 71, .H654, 1932" located at the Tennessee State Library and Archives. 31-page manuscript contains great detail on the genealogy of this branch of the Hillman family.

Hillman surname file, Tennessee State Library and Archives.

Land Between the Lakes National Recreation Area, official website:
https://www.landbetweenthelakes.us/

Land Between the Rivers, by Ed Huddleston, article reprinted from the Nashville Banner, September 1957.

Land Between the Rivers, *Chapter 3, Iron Manufacture,* by Dr. J. Milton Henry. Published 1970 by Taylor Publishing Company.

Masters of the Big House: Elite Slaveholders of the Mid-Nineteenth Century South, by William Koffman Scarborough. Louisiana State University Press. 2003. (Daniel Hillman slave ownership, page 462. Isaac Franklin slave ownership, pages 124, 125, 430, 454.)

The Monmouth County Historical Assoc.: Library and Archives Manuscripts Collection:
http://www.monmouthhistory.org/Sections-read-23.html

Nashville Union and American, Friday, April 3, 1874 (D. Hillman and Sons ad).
http://chroniclingamerica.loc.gov/lccn/sn85033699/1874-04-03/ed-1/seq-1/

Nashville Union and American, Thursday, June 25, 1874 (D. Hillman and Sons ad).
http://chroniclingamerica.loc.gov/lccn/sn85033699/1874-06-25/ed-1/seq-1/

One Century of Lyon County History, *Chapter 10—Tennessee Rolling Mill.* Lyon County Historical Society, pub. 1964.

Profiles of the Past, by Odell Walker, 1994, McClanahan Publishing House, Inc. (includes information on Lyon County, KY and Daniel Hillman)

A Sketch of the Life of Daniel Hillman, unpublished manuscript by J. B. Killebrew, read February 14th, 1886, by Judge Whitworth, before the Tennessee Historical Society. Vintage copy in the Family History Collection of Terry Martin.

Hillman, Daniel C.—Nannie's half-brother:

Ancestral Chronological Record of the Hillman Family—1550-1905, by Harry W. Hillman 1905, out of print full text appears here:
https://archive.org/stream/ancestralchronol00lchill/ancestralchronol00lchill_djvu.txt

Daniel C. Hillman, Find A Grave entry. Accessed 20 February 2018. Memorial no#178979520, citing Mount Olivet Cemetery, Nashville, Davidson County, Tennessee, USA; Maintained by vcudean (contributor 48748331): https://www.findagrave.com/cgi-bin/fg.cgi?page=gr&GRid=178979520

Hillman Family—Haddonfield, N.J., Branch—Genealogy, 1932, no author credited, 1932. "Reference CS, 71, .H654, 1932" located at the Tennessee State Library and Archives. 31-page manuscript contains great detail on the genealogy of this branch of the Hillman family.

Hillman surname file, Tennessee State Library and Archives.

Hillman, Daniel Hannold (Sr.)—Nannie's grandfather:

Ancestral Chronological Record of the Hillman Family—1550-1905, by Harry W. Hillman 1905, out of print full text appears here:
https://archive.org/stream/ancestralchronol00lchill/ancestralchronol00lchill_djvu.txt

Hillman Family—Haddonfield, N.J., Branch—Genealogy, 1932, no author credited, 1932. "Reference CS, 71, .H654, 1932" located at the Tennessee State Library and Archives. 31-page manuscript contains great detail on the genealogy of this branch of the Hillman family.

Old Tannehill: A History of the Pioneer Ironworks in Roupes Valley (1829-1865), by James R. Bennett. Published by the Jefferson County Historical Commission. 1986.

The Story of Coal and Iron in Alabama, by Ethel Armes, 1910. The University Press, Cambridge. USA. https://archive.org/stream/storyofcoaliron00arme/storyofcoaliron00arme_djvu.txt

Tannehill and the Growth of the Alabama Iron Industry, Including the Civil War in West Alabama, by James R. Bennett. 1999. Published by Alabama Historic Iron Works Commission.

Tannehill Ironworks Historical State Park, official website: *http://www.tannehill.org/*

Hillman, George Washington:

Ancestral Chronological Record of the Hillman Family—1550-1905, by Harry W. Hillman 1905, out of print full text appears here:
https://archive.org/stream/ancestralchronol00lchill/ancestralchronol00lchill_djvu.txt

The Family History Collection of Bob Claxton, Franklin, Tennessee. Bob is one of the few descendants of G. W. Hillman by way of his daughter, Martha Jane "Mattie" Hillman Ewin. His collection contains many personal and expense journals from G. W. Hillman, Capt. William G. Ewin, and Mattie Hillman Ewin.

Hillman Family—Haddonfield, N.J., Branch—Genealogy, 1932, no author credited, 1932. "Reference CS, 71, .H654, 1932" located at the Tennessee State Library and Archives. 31-page manuscript contains great detail on the genealogy of this branch of the Hillman family.

Hurricane Mills Rural Historic District, National Register of Historic Places, registration form, application dated 1999: *https://npgallery.nps.gov/GetAsset/f09a8be3-c487-478d-a4d4-b23b97c54a99*

Hillman, Henry Frazer:

Hillman Family Bible, property of Thomas D. Martin, Gallatin, Tenn. The information from this Bible can also be found online at the following link: *http://home.rootsweb.com/~tnsumner/brhillman.htm* and also at the Tennessee State Library and Archives in the Hillman surname file.

Hillman Family—Haddonfield, N.J., Branch—Genealogy, 1932, no author credited, 1932. "Reference CS, 71, .H654, 1932" located at the Tennessee State Library and Archives. 31-page manuscript contains great detail on the genealogy of this branch of the Hillman family.

Hillman, Henry Lea:

Calgon Carbon. Wikipedia: *https://en.wikipedia.org/wiki/Calgon_Carbon*

Henry Hillman, Wikipedia: *https://en.wikipedia.org/wiki/Henry_Hillman*

The Hillman Company, official website: *http://hillmancompany.com/*

Hillman Family—Haddonfield, N.J., Branch—Genealogy, 1932, no author credited, 1932. "Reference CS, 71, .H654, 1932" located at the Tennessee State Library and Archives. 31-page manuscript contains great detail on the genealogy of this branch of the Hillman family.

The Hillmans of Pittsburgh, article in Forbes, September 15, 1969, pp. 42-56. (No author credited.)

Hillman, James Hoggatt (and Knoxie Polk Walker Hillman):

Ancestral Chronological Record of the Hillman Family—1550-1905, by Harry W. Hillman 1905, out of print full text appears here:
https://archive.org/stream/ancestralchronol00lchill/ancestralchronol00lchill_djvu.txt

Hillman Family—Haddonfield, N.J., Branch—Genealogy, 1932, no author credited, 1932. "Reference CS, 71, .H654, 1932" located at the Tennessee State Library and Archives. 31-page manuscript contains great detail on the genealogy of this branch of the Hillman family.

Hillman surname file, Tennessee State Library and Archives.

James Hoggatt Hillman, Find A Grave entry. Accessed 20 February 2018. Memorial no. 55769545, citing Mount Olivet Cemetery, Nashville, Davidson County, Tennessee, USA; Maintained by Jerry G. Marable (contributor 46969784): *https://www.findagrave.com/cgi-bin/fg.cgi?page=gr&GRid=55769545*

Knoxie Polk Walker Hillman, Find A Grave entry. Accessed 21 February 2018. Memorial no. 63073026, citing Oakwood Cemetery, Montgomery, Montgomery County, Alabama, USA. Maintained by Lonewalker (contributor 46987063): *https://www.findagrave.com/memorial/63073026*

Sweet Mystery: A Book of Remembering, by Judith Hillman Paterson, Farrar, Straus, and Giroux. 1996.

Hillman, John Hartwell "Hart" (and Sallie Murfree Frazer Hillman):

Ancestral Chronological Record of the Hillman Family—1550-1905, by Harry W. Hillman 1905, out of print full text appears here:
https://archive.org/stream/ancestralchronol00lchill/ancestralchronol00lchill_djvu.txt

Hillman Family Bible, property of Thomas D. Martin, Gallatin, Tenn. The information from this Bible can also be found online at the following link: *http://home.rootsweb.com/~tnsumner/brhillman.htm* and also at the Tennessee State Library and Archives in the Hillman surname file.

Hillman Family—Haddonfield, N.J., Branch—Genealogy, 1932, no author credited, 1932. "Reference CS, 71, .H654, 1932" located at the Tennessee State Library and Archives. 31-page manuscript contains great detail on the genealogy of this branch of the Hillman family.

Hillman surname file, Tennessee State Library and Archives. *J. Hartwell Hillman, Sr.,* Wikipedia. *https://en.wikipedia.org/wiki/J._Hartwell_Hillman_Sr.*

Nashville Union and American, Friday, April 3, 1874 (D. Hillman and Sons ad).
http://chroniclingamerica.loc.gov/lccn/sn85033699/1874-04-03/ed-1/seq-1/

Nashville Union and American, Thursday, June 25, 1874 (D. Hillman and Sons ad).
http://chroniclingamerica.loc.gov/lccn/sn85033699/1874-06-25/ed-1/seq-1/

Sallie Murfree Frazer Hillman, Find A Grave entry. Accessed 20 February 2018. Memorial no. 90935892, citing Homewood Cemetery, Pittsburgh, Allegheny County, Pennsylvania, USA. Maintained by Graves (contributor 47171280): *https://www.findagrave.com/cgi-bin/fg.cgi?page=gr&GRid=90935892*

Hillman, John W. (and Ellen Putney Hillman):

The Family Research of Ursula Sheffield-Bradshaw, Cincinnati, Ohio, including DNA test analysis. Ursula is a descendant of John W. and Ellen Putney Hillman.

John W. Hillman (Chapter XXXV), Biographical Sketches of Prominent Negro Men and Women of Kentucky, by William Decker Johnson. The Standard Print, Lexington, KY. 1897. Pages 60-61, 87. Full book text on line at
https://books.google.com/books/about/Biographical_Sketches_of_Prominent_Negro.html?id=bgRAAQ AAMAAJ&printsec=frontcover&source=kp_read_button#v=onepage&q&f=false

John W. Hillman, entry appearing in Notable Kentucky African Americans Database website, *https://nkaa.uky.edu/nkaa/items/show/1110*

Hillman, Meredith Poindexter Gentry "Gentry" (and Lallie Wooldridge Hillman):

Ancestral Chronological Record of the Hillman Family—1550-1905, by Harry W. Hillman 1905, out of print full text appears here:
https://archive.org/stream/ancestralchronol00lchill/ancestralchronol00lchill_djvu.txt

Christian County Kentucky, Vol. 2, a family history volume compiled by Lon Bostick, Turner Publishing Company, 1991, page 269 (Lallie Wooldridge and Gentry Hillman).
https://books.google.com/books?id=OOEQpGl-mukC&pg=PA269&lpg=PA269&dq=%22Gentry+Hillman%22&source=bl&ots=7JgkWBGbd6&sig=9wWC7wvvkV-uXkDZjLH1N1VmctA&hl=en&sa=X&ved=0ahUKEwi2t8361YfXAhVl2IMKHSoSC704ChDoAQhCMAc#v=onepage&q=%22Gentry%20Hillman%22&f=false

Hillman Family—Haddonfield, N.J., Branch—Genealogy, 1932, no author credited, 1932. "Reference CS, 71, .H654, 1932" located at the Tennessee State Library and Archives. 31-page manuscript contains great detail on the genealogy of this branch of the Hillman family.

Hillman surname file, Tennessee State Library and Archives.

Meredith Poindexter Gentry Hillman, Find A Grave entry. Accessed 20 February 2018. Memorial no. 87836957, citing Cypress Lawn Memorial Park, Colma, San Mateo County, California, USA; Maintained by Graves (contributor 47171280): *https://www.findagrave.com/cgi-bin/fg.cgi?page=gr&GRid=87836957*

Hillman, Thomas Tennessee: (For wife, Emily Gentry Hillman, see 'Gentry Family'.)

Ancestral Chronological Record of the Hillman Family—1550-1905, by Harry W. Hillman 1905, out of print full text appears here:
https://archive.org/stream/ancestralchronol00lchill/ancestralchronol00lchill_djvu.txt

The Family History Collection of Terry Martin, Gallatin, Tennessee. Contains a large number of obituaries of T. T. Hillman cut out from newspapers by Nannie.

Hillman Family—Haddonfield, N.J., Branch—Genealogy, 1932, no author credited, 1932. "Reference CS, 71, .H654, 1932" located at the Tennessee State Library and Archives. 31-page manuscript contains great detail on the genealogy of this branch of the Hillman family.

Hillman surname file, Tennessee State Library and Archives.

Hillman, Thomas Tennessee file, Tennessee State Library and Archives.

Jefferson County and Birmingham, Alabama: Historical and Biographical. 1887. Chapter X—Pioneer Iron Makers and Iron Interests, by John Witherspoon DuBose:
https://books.google.com/books?id=K2QTAAAAYAAJ&pg=PA587&lpg=PA587&dq=%22Dr.+E.+N.+Franklin%22&source=bl&ots=CYgEK9zcDq&sig=dkAgOs383Op9yfyuptWdmNW13k8&hl=en&sa=X&ved=0ahUKEwiIvpX-

iqTUAhVOziYKHWZaAwcQ6AEIRzAG#v=onepage&q=%22Dr.%20E.%20N.%20Franklin%22&f=false

Nashville Union and American, Friday, April 3, 1874 (D. Hillman and Sons ad).
http://chroniclingamerica.loc.gov/lccn/sn85033699/1874-04-03/ed-1/seq-1/

Nashville Union and American, Thursday, June 25, 1874 (D. Hillman and Sons ad).
http://chroniclingamerica.loc.gov/lccn/sn85033699/1874-06-25/ed-1/seq-1/

The Story of Coal and Iron in Alabama, by Ethel Armes, 1910. The University Press, Cambridge. USA.
https://archive.org/stream/storyofcoalironi00arme/storyofcoalironi00arme_djvu.txt

Tannehill and the Growth of the Alabama Iron Industry, Including the Civil War in West Alabama, by James R. Bennett. 1999. Published by Alabama Historic Iron Works Commission.

Thomas Tennessee Hillman, Find A Grave entry. Accessed 20 February 2018. Memorial no. 7358913, citing Mount Olivet Cemetery, Nashville, Davidson County, Tennessee, USA. Maintained by Find A Grave (contributor 8): *https://www.findagrave.com/memorial/7358913/thomas-tennessee-hillman*

Thomas Tennessee Hillman Managed 2 Furnaces, by David Buck. Article appeared in The Cadiz Record, Thursday, October 25, 1984.

House Family (Allen Luke Palmer House and Grace Franklin House):

Allen Luke Palmer House, Find A Grave entry. Accessed 20 February 2018. Memorial no. 65478145, citing Gallatin City Cemetery, Gallatin, Sumner County, Tennessee, USA. Maintained by Jean Wilkerson (contributor 47306307): *https://www.findagrave.com/memorial/65478145/allen_luke-palmer-house*

General Jethro Sumner Chapter NSDAR Gallatin, Tennessee. Grace Franklin House cited as 1st Regent on the history page. Website: *http://www.tndar.org/~jethrosumner/wp/sample-page/chapter-history/*

Grace Franklin House, Find A Grave entry. Accessed 20 February 2018. Memorial no. 136543881, citing Mount Olivet Cemetery, Nashville, Davidson County, Tennessee, USA. Maintained by Jerry G. Marable (contributor 46969784): *https://www.findagrave.com/memorial/136543881/grace-house*

Hillman Family Bible, property of Thomas D. Martin, Gallatin, Tenn. The information from this Bible can also be found online at the following link: *http://home.rootsweb.com/~tnsumner/brhillman.htm* and also at the Tennessee State Library and Archives in the Hillman surname file.

Hillman Family—Haddonfield, N.J., Branch—Genealogy, 1932, no author credited, 1932. "Reference CS, 71, .H654, 1932" located at the Tennessee State Library and Archives. 31-page manuscript contains great detail on the genealogy of this branch of the Hillman family.

Jarman Family (Walton Maxey Jarman and Sarah McFerrin Anderson Jarman):

Hillman Family Bible, property of Thomas D. Martin, Gallatin, Tenn. The information from this Bible can also be found online at the following link: *http://home.rootsweb.com/~tnsumner/brhillman.htm* and also at the Tennessee State Library and Archives in the Hillman surname file.

Hillman Family—Haddonfield, N.J., Branch—Genealogy, 1932, no author credited, 1932. "Reference CS, 71, .H654, 1932" located at the Tennessee State Library and Archives. 31-page manuscript contains great detail on the genealogy of this branch of the Hillman family.

Miss Sarah McFerrin Anderson Weds Maxey Jarman at Gallatin Ceremony, The Nashville Tennessean, Thursday, October 11, 1928, p. 9.

Rites Tomorrow for Civic Leader Sarah Jarman, The Tennessean, Friday, March 21, 1997, p. 21.

Walton Maxey Jarman, Find A Grave entry. Accessed 20 February 2018. Memorial no. 46236752, citing Mount Olivet Cemetery, Nashville, Davidson County, Tennessee, USA. Maintained by Tom Childers (contributor 46515204): *https://www.findagrave.com/memorial/46236752/walton-maxey-jarman*

Kirkpatrick Family (John Beeman Kirkpatrick II and Nannie "Nan" Franklin Kirkpatrick):

Hillman Family Bible, property of Thomas D. Martin, Gallatin, Tenn. The information from this Bible can also be found online at the following link: *http://home.rootsweb.com/~tnsumner/brhillman.htm* and also at the Tennessee State Library and Archives in the Hillman surname file.

Hillman Family—Haddonfield, N.J., Branch—Genealogy, 1932, no author credited, 1932. "Reference CS, 71, .H654, 1932" located at the Tennessee State Library and Archives. 31-page manuscript contains great detail on the genealogy of this branch of the Hillman family.

Nannie Franklin "Nan" Kirkpatrick, Memorial page, Hamlin & Hilbish Funeral Directors website: *http://www.hamlinhilbish.com/obituaries/Nannie-Kirkpatrick/#!/Obituary*

Lea, John M.:

A School for the Blind was Established, by E.D. Thomson, article appearing on "The News" website for February 17, 2016: *http://www.gcanews.com/a-school-for-the-blind-was-established/*

Maddin, Dr.:

Two Worthy Men Gone, (the death of the Drs. Maddin) The Tennessean, May 5, 1908, p. 4. *https://www.newspapers.com/newspage/118817077/*

Marable Family:

Ann Jones Marable Hillman, Find A Grave entry. Accessed 20 February 2018. Memorial no. 19715495, citing Marable Cemetery, Clarksville, Montgomery County, Tennessee, USA. Maintained by REALTORINAZ (contributor 48628101): *https://www.findagrave.com/memorial/19715495/ann-jones-hillman*

The Family History Collection of Grace Paine Terzian, Washington, D.C. For use in the current volume were research notes and records on sundry Hillman and Marable relatives, research gathered by Grace's mother, Grace Benedict Paine.

The Historic Sam Davis Home and Plantation, official website: *http://www.samdavishome.org/*

John Hartwell Marable, Wikipedia. *https://en.wikipedia.org/wiki/John_Hartwell_Marable*

Marable Family History, website: *http://www.marable-family.net/jlmarable/index.html*

Martin-Hewitt Facebook messaging conversation on May 17, 2017 between the editor and Site Interpreter "Hewitt," to determine status of the Rev. Henry Hartwell Marable log cabin on the grounds at the Historic Sam Davis Home and Plantation. Hewitt confirmed that it will someday be restored and used as interpretive space.

Martin Family (Oscar E. Martin and Allen Palmer House Martin):

Allen Palmer House Martin, Find A Grave entry. Accessed 20 February 2018. Memorial no. 73518295, citing Laurel Dale Cemetery (Rugby), Scott County, Tennessee, USA. Maintained by Melissa Bertram Daugherty (contributor 47556981): *https://www.findagrave.com/memorial/73518295/allen-palmer-martin*

The Family History Collection of Terry Martin, Gallatin, Tennessee. For use in the current volume, aside from many vintage photographs, letters and letterheads, invitations and lists, there are included a number of saved obituaries from vintage papers, financial records, receipts, letters from various Hillman relatives, volumes of Nannie's music from school, and other Hillman and Franklin items, saved by Nannie Hillman Franklin, passed down through the family to Martin.

Hillman Family Bible, property of Thomas D. Martin, Gallatin, Tenn. The information from this Bible can also be found online at the following link: *http://home.rootsweb.com/~tnsumner/brhillman.htm* and also at the Tennessee State Library and Archives in the Hillman surname file.

Hillman Family—Haddonfield, N.J., Branch—Genealogy, 1932, no author credited, 1932. "Reference CS, 71, .H654, 1932" located at the Tennessee State Library and Archives. 31-page manuscript contains great detail on the genealogy of this branch of the Hillman family.

Rugby Grateful for One Man's Vision, The Tennessean, Wednesday, April 20, 1988, p. 57.

Services Today for Oscar E. Martin, 95, The Tennessean, Saturday, June 16, 1990, p. 51.

Maxwell House Hotel:

Maxwell House Hotel, Wikipedia. *https://en.wikipedia.org/wiki/Maxwell_House_Hotel*

Murfree Family:

Mary Noailles Murfree, Notable American Women, 1607-1950: A Biographical Dictionary, Volume 1, edited by Edward T. James. Radcliffe College 1971. Page 602: *https://books.google.com/books?id=rVLOhGt1BX0C&pg=RA1-PA602&lpg=RA1-PA602&dq=%22Chegaray+Institute%22&source=bl&ots=mcuLfPPcil&sig=KdnB4A5vFPcvEuILgEi83zz0zRw&hl=en&sa=X&ved=0ahUKEwiBwtz6247XAhUF8IMKHWQvCuE4ChDoAQgnMAA#v=onepage&q=%22Chegaray%20Institute%22&f=false*

Mary Noailles Murfree, Wikipedia. *https://en.wikipedia.org/wiki/Mary_Noailles_Murfree*

The Murfree Family, Grantlands Project website page: *https://grantlandsproject.omeka.net/exhibits/show/rediscovering-grantlands/family/the-murfree-family*

Sallie Murfree Frazer Hillman, Find A Grave entry. Accessed 20 February 2018. Memorial no. 90935892, citing Homewood Cemetery, Pittsburgh, Allegheny County, Pennsylvania, USA. Maintained by Graves (contributor 47171280): *https://www.findagrave.com/cgi-bin/fg.cgi?page=gr&GRid=90935892*

See also mentions in newspaper articles in Appendix 2.

Noel Family:

Florida Mercer Noel Franklin, Find A Grave entry. Accessed 20 February 2018. Memorial no. 23381674, citing Frankfort Cemetery, Frankfort, Franklin County, Kentucky, USA. Maintained by Ken (contributor 46953017): *https://www.findagrave.com/memorial/23381674/florida-mercer-franklin*

History of Kentucky Baptists, Vol. 1, authored and published by John Henderson Spencer, 1885. Bio of Silas Mercer Noel, pp. 316-319, as excerpted on History of the Restoration Movement webpage: *http://www.therestorationmovement.com/_states/kentucky/noel,silas,m.htm*

Maria Waring Noel, Find A Grave entry. Accessed 20 February 2018. Memorial no. 23381552, citing Frankfort Cemetery, Frankfort, Franklin County, Kentucky, USA. Maintained by Ken (contributor 46953017): *https://www.findagrave.com/memorial/23381552/maria-noel*

Silas Mercer Noel, 1913 biographical essay by Frederick W. Eberhardt, D. D., appearing on Baptist History Homepage: *http://baptisthistoryhomepage.com/noel.s.m.html*

Rev. Silas Mercer Noel, Find A Grave entry. Accessed 20 February 2018. Memorial no. 23021764, citing Frankfort Cemetery, Frankfort, Franklin County, Kentucky, USA. Maintained by Ken (contributor 46953017): *https://www.findagrave.com/memorial/23021764/silas-mercer-noel*

Phrenology (and Professor O. S. Fowler):

Phrenological Character of Miss Ann Fredonia Hillman, by O. S. Fowler. New Orleans, Feb. 8th, 1859. William Giles, Reporter. Original handwritten 9-page document in the Family History Collection of Terry L. Martin.

Thomas Hughes Free Public Library, Rugby, Tennessee. The historic library contains only volumes predating 1900. Two of Nannie Hillman Franklin's French books were donated in the past to the library. Also noted for the purposes of the research are the many volumes on Phrenology.

The Fowler Brothers: "Know Thyself". No author credited. On View: Curated content from the Center for History of Medicine's extraordinary collections. The Francis A. Countway Library of Medicine, website page: *https://collections.countway.harvard.edu/onview/exhibits/show/talking-heads/the-fowler-brothers*

Porter Family:

Funeral Services Set For A. J. Porter, Sr., The Tennessean, Nashville, Tennessee, Feb. 20, 1949. *https://www.newspapers.com/clip/10208218/the_tennessean/*

Lady in Gray: Martha Watson Porter Still Roaming at Riverwood, by Grace Benedict Paine, article appearing in The Historic Register For the Appreciation and Preservation of Nashville's Past Sponsored by Historic Nashville, Inc.,Vol. 5, Spring 1984, attached to RootsWeb website entry "Todd County Kentucky Pioneers, Andersons, and Watsons": *http://wc.rootsweb.ancestry.com/cgi-bin/igm.cgi?op=GET&db=toddcountyky&id=I6289*

Porter, Alexander James, The Biographical Dictionary of America, Vol. 08, page 390. Wikisource website page: *https://en.wikisource.org/wiki/Page:The_Biographical_Dictionary_of_America,_vol._08.djvu/390*

Rebecca Greer Allison (Porter), Ancestry website page: *https://www.ancestry.com/genealogy/records/rebecca-greer-allison_45955751*

Tennessee Portrait Projects, website (Alexander James Porter) *http://tnportraits.org/porter-alexander-james.htm*

See also mentions in newspaper articles in Appendix 2.

Rock City:

Nashville's Historical Timeline, Nashville Encyclopedia website page: *http://www.nashville.gov/Encyclopedia/Timeline.aspx*

Scales Family (David Campbell Scales and Grace Cora Hillman Scales):

Ancestral Chronological Record of the Hillman Family—1550-1905, by Harry W. Hillman 1905, out of print full text appears here:
https://archive.org/stream/ancestralchronol00lchill/ancestralchronol00lchill_djvu.txt

The Family History Collection of Grace Paine Terzian, Washington, D.C. For use in the current volume were research notes and records on sundry Hillman relatives, including Daniel Hillman, David Campbell Scales and Grace Hillman Scales, research gathered by Grace's mother, Grace Benedict Paine.

Hillman Family Bible, property of Thomas D. Martin, Gallatin, Tenn. The information from this Bible can also be found online at the following link: *http://home.rootsweb.com/~tnsumner/brhillman.htm* and also at the Tennessee State Library and Archives in the Hillman surname file.

Hillman Family—Haddonfield, N.J., Branch—Genealogy, 1932, no author credited, 1932. "Reference CS, 71, .H654, 1932" located at the Tennessee State Library and Archives. 31-page manuscript contains great detail on the genealogy of this branch of the Hillman family.

Hillman surname file, Tennessee State Library and Archives.
McFerrin Park and the Bryan-McFerrin-Scales House, Nashville History website:
http://nashvillehistory.blogspot.com/2012/01/mcferrin-park-and-bryan-mcferrin-scales.html

Sheafe, Charles A.:

Captain Charles A. Sheafe, bio mention on page 177 in Annals of the Army of the Cumberland… originally published Philadelphia. Lippincott 1863. Full text here:
https://archive.org/stream/annalsofarmyofcu00websuoft/annalsofarmyofcu00websuoft_djvu.txt

Capt. Charles A. Sheafe, Find A Grave entry. Accessed 20 February 2018. Memorial no. 146756253, citing Hillsboro Cemetery, Hillsboro, Highland County, Ohio, USA. Maintained by Jay Wright (contributor 47711501): *https://www.findagrave.com/cgi-bin/fg.cgi?page=gr&GRid=146756253*

Charles A. Sheafe, bio mention on page 75 of *Stones River, Creating a Battlefield Park 1863-1932,* dissertation by John Riley George, 2013.
http://jewlscholar.mtsu.edu/bitstream/handle/mtsu/3669/George_mtsu_0170E_10078.pdf?sequence

Fishing Rod Holder, patented by Charles A. Sheafe in 1890. Google Patents website:
http://www.google.com.pg/patents/US440727

See also mentions in newspaper articles in Appendix 2.

Van Bibber Family (George Lindenberger Van Bibber and Adele Franklin Van Bibber):

Franklin surname file, Sumner County Archives. (A letter in this file is from Adele to her father from her school in Nashville.)

George Lindenberger Van Bibber, (husband to Adele Franklin) Find A Grave entry. Accessed 19 February 2018, Memorial no. 98680935, citing Churchville Presbyterian Church Cemetery, Churchville, Harford County, Maryland, USA; Maintained by John Dowdy (contributor 47791572):
https://www.findagrave.com/cgi-bin/fg.cgi?page=gr&GSln=Van+Bibber&GSfn=George&GSbyrel=all&GSdyrel=all&GSob=n&GRid=98680935&df=all&

Van Bibber family scrapbook, put together by Armfield Franklin Van Bibber (a son of Edward's sister, Adele Franklin Van Bibber), in the possession of descendant W. T. (Tom) Whitney of South Paris, Maine. Certain information on the Archers and the Van Bibbers came from this.

See also newspaper articles in Appendix 1.

Waugh, Samuel Bell:

Samuel Waugh, Wikipedia. *https://en.wikipedia.org/wiki/Samuel_Waugh*

Winston Family (J. D. Winston and daughter Jennie Winston):

Beersheba Springs, Grundy County, Tenn. (advertisement), Nashville Union and American, Nashville, Tenn., Saturday, May 13, 1871.

The Family Chronicle and Kinship Book of Maclin, Clack, Cocke, Carter, Taylor, Cross, Gordon and Other Related American Lineages, by Octavia Zollicoffer Bond, bio of *Joseph Woods Gordon*, p. 317. (Ed. note. Despite the presented information, Jennie Winston was the daughter of Dr. J. D. Winston, not Dr. W. K. Winston.)
https://books.google.com/books?id=6uE1AAAAMAAJ&pg=PA317&lpg=PA317&dq=%22Joseph+Woods+Gordon%22+Jennie&source=bl&ots=IwsxiT9H7i&sig=dsW_ibAbZMZWWS1a7XYBUrSsxog&hl=en&sa=X&ved=0ahUKEwi2xZemxbXZAhUM6oMKHWdyCekQ6AEILzAD#v=onepage&q=%22Joseph%20Woods%20Gordon%22%20Jennie&f=false

Nashville Union and American, Sunday, January 7, 1872 (Jennie Winston marriage announcement). *https://www.newspapers.com/newspage/80855804/*

See also mentions in newspaper articles in Appendix 2.

Yerger, William:

Judge William Yerger, Find A Grave entry. Accessed 20 February 2018. Memorial no. 117201550, citing Greenwood Cemetery, Jackson, Hinds County, Mississippi, USA. Maintained by Linda Thompson (contributor 47749170): *https://www.findagrave.com/cgi-bin/fg.cgi?page=gr&GRid=117201550*

See also mentions in newspaper articles in Appendix 2.

For Further Reading

Adelicia: Grace, Grit, and Gumption, by Joyce Blaylock. 2017. Parnassus Books. ----*A Historical novel about Adelicia Hayes Franklin Acklen Cheatham, one of the south's most interesting women.* (Must be special-ordered by Parnassus Books in Nashville.)

Beersheba Springs, a History: Volume I. General History, the Hotel-Assembly, and Shops, edited by Clopper Almon. 2010. Beersheba Springs Historical Society. (Still in Print. Can be purchased in the Beersheba Springs Museum or on their website.)

Beersheba Springs, a History: Volume II. Families, Homes, Lore, and More, edited by Clopper Almon. 2010. Beersheba Springs Historical Society. (Still in Print. Can be purchased in the Beersheba Springs Museum or on their website.)

Beersheba Springs, a History: Volume III. Classics, edited by Clopper Almon, 2011. Beersheba Springs Historical Society. (Still in Print. Can be purchased in the Beersheba Springs Museum or on their website.)

The Beersheba Springs Diaries of L. Virginia French, edited by Herschel Gower. Beersheba Springs Historical Society. 1986. (Still in Print. Can be purchased in the Beersheba Springs Museum or on their website.)

The Diary of Nannie Haskins Williams: A Southern Woman's Story of Rebellion and Reconstruction, 1863-1890, edited by Minoa D. Uffelman, Ellen Kanervo, Phyllis Smith, and Eleanor Williams. University of Tennessee Press. 2014. ----*This diary was repeatedly used with voice-overs in the PBS miniseries, "The Civil War," produced by Ken Burns. Nannie and her cousin Mattie are mentioned several times in the published diary.* (Still in print, widely available.)

Flush Times and Fever Dreams: A Story of Capitalism and Slavery in the Age of Jackson, by Joshua D. Rothman. University of Georgia Press. 2012. (Still in print, widely available.)

The Half Has Never Been Told: Slavery and the Making of American Capitalism, by Edward E. Baptist. Basic Books. 2014. (Still in print, widely available.)

Images of America: Around Gallatin and Sumner County, by Dee Gee Lester and Kenneth Calvin Thomson, Jr. Arcadia Publishing. 1998. ---- *This is a pictorial history of Sumner County up through the 1920s.* (Currently out of print. Can be found on used book websites.)

Images of America: Around Gallatin and Sumner County-Volume II, by Dee Gee Lester and Kenneth Calvin Thomson, Jr. Arcadia Publishing. 1998. ----*This is a pictorial history of Sumner County from the 1920s to 1960.* (Still in print. Can be found in Middle Tennessee area bookstores.)

John Armfield of Beersheba Springs, by Isabel Howell. 2011 reprint of 1943 and 1944 articles. Beersheba Springs Historical Society. (Still in print. Can be found at the Beersheba Springs Museum or on their website.)

Old Sumner: A History of Sumner County Tennessee from 1805-1861, by Walter T. Durham. Published by the Sumner County Library Board. 1972. (Out of print. Can be found on used book websites or in some libraries in Middle Tennessee.)

Old Tannehill: A History of the Pioneer Ironworks in Roupes Valley (1829-1865), by James R. Bennett. Published by the Jefferson County Historical Commission. 1986. (Still in print. Can be purchased at Tannehill Ironworks Historical State Park.)

Slaves in the Family, by Edward Ball. 1998. Farrar, Straus, and Giroux. ----*About the author's slave-owning families on the rice plantations of South Carolina.* (Still in print, widely available.)

Sweet Mystery: A Book of Remembering, by Judith Hillman Paterson. Farrar, Straus, and Giroux. 1996. Newer editions by University of Alabama Press ----*Author is a descendant of James Hoggatt Hillman, a son of Daniel Hillman and Mary Gentry Hillman, and half-brother to Nannie. This biography tells a bit of the tale of this branch of the Hillman family.* (Still in print. Can be purchased on Amazon.com.)

Tannehill and the Growth of the Alabama Iron Industry, Including the Civil War in West Alabama, by James R. Bennett. 1999. Published by Alabama Historic Iron Works Commission. (Still in print. Can be purchased at Tannehill Ironworks Historical State Park.)

Index

absent friend, 20
Acklen, Joseph, 10, 90
Adams, John (of Beersheba Springs), 146
Adams, John Quincy, 5
Adkins, Heather, 46
Alexandria, Virginia, 4, 8, 139
Alice, 9, 12, 40, 76, 96, 116, 119, 120, 121, 125
Alice Furnaces, 7
all went merry as a marriage bell, 20
Allen, Jennie, 50, 133
Allen, Louis, 84
Allison Family, 49, 57
Allison, Alethea, 50, 63, 133, 138
Almon, Clopper, 146
alone to weep the silent tear, 21
Anderson Family, 75, 76, 77, 79
Anderson, Florida Franklin, 75, 76, 77, 78, 104, 109, 113
Anderson, Grace Adele, 77, 78, 109
Anderson, Nannie Hillman, 76, 78
Anderson, Walter Leake, 76, 78, 104, 109
Appomattox, 12, 40, 96
Archer, Jane Cage "Blanche" Franklin, 9, 10, 12, 46, 93, 124
Archer, Stevenson, 9, 11, 12, 46
Arlington National Cemetery, 79, 113
Armfield Cemetery, 34, 93
Armfield estate, 76, 142
Armfield Family, 5, 8, 11, 12, 93
Armfield home, 11, 15, 25, 34, 93
Armfield, John, 3, 4, 8, 9, 10, 11, 12, 15, 22, 26, 29, 30, 34, 36, 38, 40, 46, 59, 70, 75, 76, 90, 91, 93, 96, 97, 99, 110, 116, 117, 119, 120, 121, 124, 137, 138, 139, 141, 142, 143, 145
Armfield, Martha Franklin, 8, 9, 10, 22, 23, 24, 26, 31, 35, 40, 42, 44, 45, 46, 47, 48, 52, 54, 59, 60, 66, 93, 97, 99, 110, 139, 140, 143
Atlanta, Georgia, 55
Baber Family, 11
Baber, John T., 116
Baber, Thomas A., 116
Baltimore, Maryland, 23, 45, 46, 52, 97, 99, 139
Banks, A.D. (Maj.), 31, 48, 138
Barbour, Caldwell "Kit", 88

Barbour, Mary Ann Hillman, 6, 88
Barrow, Judge, 138
Barrows, Miss, 133
Bass Cottage, 34
Bass, John Meredith, 34, 138
Bate, William B. (Gen.), 42
Battle Creek, Tennessee, 21, 27, 31
beacon light, 32
Beersheba Springs Historical Society, 31, 146
Beersheba Springs Hotel, 11, 20, 21, 27, 30, 35, 36, 37, 110, 131, 132, 135, 137, 138, 139
Beersheba Springs Museum, 31
Beersheba Springs, Tennessee, 4, 11, 15, 16, 17, 19, 20, 21, 24, 26, 31, 32, 34, 36, 44, 46, 49, 51, 79, 93, 97, 98, 110, 111, 131, 132, 134, 137, 149, 168
Bel Air, Maryland, 12, 23, 46, 97, 116, 121
Bell Buckle, Tennessee, 77, 105
Bell, B. D., 118, 124
Bell, Dick (Col.), 138
Belmont Mansion, 10, 11, 90, 146
Birmingham, Alabama, 4, 5, 7, 86
Blackmore, James W., 118, 119
Blue Grass Country Club, 93
Bond, Minnie, 39
Borcher, Charles Allen, 78, 79, 109
Borcher, Florida Noel Franklin, 78, 79, 110
Borcher, Tom, 145
Bowman, Teresa, 146
Branch, Theola, 133, 136
Breffeihl, Cherie, 145
Brown, Joe, 134, 136
Brown, John C. (Gen.), 39
Brown, Mark, 146
Brown, Mrs., 138
Brown, W. L., 31, 138
Buck, Miss, 138
Buford, Edward L., 64, 136
Burton, Annie, 133, 136
Burton, John W. (Col.), 138
Burton, Miss, 138
Burton, Mrs., 138
Burwell, Blanche Franklin, 9
Calgon Carbon, 7, 85
Calhoun, John C., 82
Campbellism movement, 10
Carter, Duncan F., 138

171

Carter, Mrs., 138
Castalian Springs, Tennessee, 114
Center Furnace, 89
Chadwell, Emma, 133
Chadwell, Mollie, 133, 135
Chattanooga, Tennessee, 42, 131, 132, 139
Cheatham, Adelicia Hayes Franklin Acklen, 8, 9, 11, 79, 90, 91, 144
Cheatham, Benjamin F. (Gen.), 39
Cheatham, Mr., 57
Cheatham, William Archer, 90
Chegaray Institute, 14, 84
Christ Church (Episcopal), Nashville, 74
Cincinnati, Ohio, 31, 46, 47, 52
Civil War, 3, 4, 5, 11, 14, 16, 93, 110, 141
Claiborne Mansion, 24
Clark & Bass, 27
Clark, Richard, 21, 26, 27, 28
Clarksville, Tennessee, 5, 14, 81, 83
Claxton, Bob, 145
Claxton, Joe, 145
Clay, Henry, 82
Coldwell, W. B., 134, 136, 137
Columbia Female Institute, 104, 105
Columbia Herald, The--newspaper, 132
Columbia, Tennessee, 57, 104, 105, 132
Comer House, 10
Confederate Army, 11, 12, 91
Confederate Veteran--magazine, 107
Cooper, Judge, 39, 98
Cooper, Miss, 133
Cooper, Washington B., 90
Correy, Rebecca, 133, 138
Craddock, Charles Egbert, 50, 84
Craighead, James Brown, 50
Craighead, Thomas D., 138
Cumberland Plateau, 11, 111, 114, 131, 138
Cumberland River, 98
Cunningham, Mrs., 138
D. Hillman & Sons, 89
D.A.R. (General Jethro Sumner Chapter), 8, 77
Dahlgreen, Gen., 138
Dahlgren, Col., 139
Davidson County, 5, 52, 98
Disappointment sinks the heart of man, 63
Dodge, John W., 90
Don Pedro (horse), 23, 26
Doty House, 28
Douglass, Dixie, 137
Douglass, Mrs., 138
drug addiction, 77, 105, 107
drummer, 12, 96

Earls, Cindy, 145
Elder, Lizzie, 133, 135, 138
Ellicott City, Maryland, 12
Ellis, W. J. (Rev.), 74
Elliston, Lizinka, 64
Elliston, Mrs., 138
Emmanuel Church, 75, 106
Empire Iron Works, 3, 23, 30, 31, 33, 34, 36, 39, 41, 66, 89
Episcopal Church, 74, 75
Escape, 81
Evans, Maggie, 133, 138
Evans, Sallie, 133, 138
Eve, Paul Fitzsimmons (Dr.), 55
Ewin, Martha Hillman, 6, 20, 51, 52, 53, 56, 58, 62, 63, 64, 66, 71, 84, 98
Ewin, William G. (Capt.), 6, 14, 52, 53, 59, 64, 98
Ewing, Robert, 24, 134, 137
Examiner, The--newspaper, 15, 16, 97, 115, 117, 118, 137, 143
Fairvue plantation, 8, 11, 90, 91, 116, 117, 121, 144
Flemming, E. F., 137
Forbes--magazine, 85
Forest Home Academy, 15
Foster, Will, 134, 136
Fowler, O. S. (Professor), 13
Foxland Hall, 11
Frankfort, Kentucky, 10, 91, 92
Franklin and Armfield, 4, 8, 90, 93
Franklin Family, 3, 5, 9, 10, 78, 79
Franklin Family Tree, 9, 78
Franklin v. Franklin, 4, 76, 115, 117, 119, 120, 122, 143
Franklin, Alexandrine (Didine) Groslevin, 78, 79, 106, 109
Franklin, Benjamin Hallowell, 9
Franklin, Charles Hillman, 75, 78, 79, 104, 109, 110, 113
Franklin, Daniel Hillman, 75, 77, 78, 79, 104, 105, 107, 113
Franklin, Dr. John Washington, 9, 10, 11, 12, 26, 42, 70, 74, 75, 76, 91, 92, 93, 94, 97, 99, 113, 115, 117, 118, 119, 120, 124, 125, 139, 142
Franklin, Edward Noel, 3, 6, 8, 9, 10, 15, 16, 51, 52, 74, 75, 76, 77, 78, 79, 88, 91, 92, 94, 95, 98, 100, 101, 102, 103, 104, 105, 107, 108, 110, 111, 112, 113, 114, 115, 116, 117, 118, 119, 120, 131, 134, 136, 141, 142, 146

Franklin, Edward Noel, Jr., 75, 78, 104, 106, 113
Franklin, Elizabeth Cage, 9, 10
Franklin, Elizabeth Rawlings, 9, 52, 99
Franklin, Ernest, 113
Franklin, Ernest (half-brother of Edward), 9
Franklin, Florida Mercer Noel, 9, 10, 91, 92, 94, 115, 120
Franklin, Isaac, 8, 9, 11, 38, 90, 91, 93, 116, 117, 121, 139, 141, 143, 144, 145
Franklin, James, 8, 9, 52, 79, 90
Franklin, James W., 9
Franklin, John, 9, 10, 46, 52, 93, 99
Franklin, John Armfield, 9, 10, 12, 40, 67, 70, 75, 76, 91, 94, 96, 115, 116, 117, 118, 119, 120, 121, 122, 124, 125, 128, 142
Franklin, Kentucky, 71
Franklin, Lina, 9
Franklin, Lucien Baber, Sr., 9
Franklin, Mabel, 9
Franklin, Mary Lauderdale, 8, 9, 52, 90
Franklin, Matilda, 46, 99, 141
Franklin, Nannie Marable, 75, 76, 78, 104, 106, 113
Franklin, Robert Lee, 9
Franklin, Sarah Baber, 9, 11, 79, 91, 92, 113, 116, 118
Franklin, Smith Claiborne, 9, 10
Franklin, Thomas Baber, 9
Frazer, Henry S., 62
Freeland, Miss, 133
Frierson, Duncan E., 138
Fulier, Andrew J., 136
Fuller, Mr., 134
Gallatin City Cemetery, 77, 91, 93, 96, 113
Gallatin Nursing Home, 77, 103
Gallatin, Tennessee, 8, 10, 15, 26, 42, 51, 52, 70, 74, 75, 76, 77, 83, 86, 90, 91, 92, 93, 97, 103, 104, 105, 108, 109, 113, 115, 116, 117, 118, 119, 120, 121, 122, 137, 143
Galveston, Texas, 15, 95
Gardner, Nat, 134, 136
Gate City Hospital, 55
Genesco, 77, 109
Gentry Family, 5
Gentry Family Bible, 87
Gentry, Emily Saunders, 87
Gentry, Meredith Poindexter, 7, 87
Georgetown College, 10, 116, 120
Gillespie, R. K., 117, 118, 119, 123
Golden Era Plantation, 90
Goodrich, Jane Hillman, 6

Goodrich, Justus Buck, 6
Gordon, Joseph Woods, 57
Gothic Revival, 92
Grace Street, 34, 86
Gray, George S., 134, 137
Gray, Jeff, 145
Greig's Bakery and Confectionary, 73
Grundy County, 3, 12, 124, 131, 149, 168
Guild, Josephus Conn (Judge), 42, 91
Guild, Walter Josephus, 42
Halbrooks Family, 82
Handley, Ross, 134, 136
Harding, T. J. (Dr.), 138
Hardwig, William (Dr.), 84, 146
Harriett, 46
Harrison, William Henry, 82
Hayes, Rutherford B. (Pres. and Mrs.), 103
Hayes, Sallie, 133, 136
Hays, Addison, 137
Head, Charles R., 117, 118, 119
Hearts that love can never remain silent, 61
Heiman, Adolphus, 88, 92
Hendersonville, Tennessee, 8, 11, 70, 93
Hicks, Olah, 133, 136
Hicks, S. W. (Col.), 138
Hillman Coal and Coke Company, 85
Hillman Company (The), 7, 85
Hillman Family, 3, 4, 5, 6, 7
Hillman Family Tree, 6
Hillman, Ann Jones Marable, 5, 6, 7, 13, 81, 82, 83, 86, 114
Hillman, Bellfield Carter, 6, 87
Hillman, Bros. and Sons, 54
Hillman, Charles Ellis, 6, 54, 81, 106
Hillman, Daniel (Jr., Nannie's father), 5, 6, 7, 13, 23, 31, 52, 54, 74, 75, 81, 83, 85, 86, 87, 88, 89, 113, 142, 145
Hillman, Daniel (Sr., Nannie's grandfather), 5, 6, 81
Hillman, Daniel C. (Nannie's half-brother), 6, 87
Hillman, Ellen Putney, 88
Hillman, Emily Gentry, 6, 7, 43, 45, 47, 86, 113
Hillman, George Washington, 6, 14, 52, 81, 98
Hillman, Grace Huston Haines, 6, 81, 86
Hillman, Henry Frazer, 59, 63
Hillman, Henry Lea, 85
Hillman, James, 6
Hillman, James Hoggatt, 6, 87
Hillman, John Hartwell (Hart), 6, 7, 50, 59, 62, 63, 85, 86, 87, 108

Hillman, John W., 6, 88
Hillman, Knoxie Polk Walker, 87
Hillman, Lallie Wooldridge, 87
Hillman, Mary Gentry, 6, 7, 47, 73, 74, 75,
    86, 87, 88, 113
Hillman, Meredith Poindexter Gentry, 6, 87
Hillman, Nannie (Ann Fredonia), 3, 6, 7, 8, 9,
    13, 15, 16, 73, 74, 75, 76, 77, 78, 79, 83,
    85, 86, 88, 97, 98, 100, 101, 102, 103,
    104, 105, 107, 108, 110, 111, 113, 114,
    115, 118, 121, 138, 141, 142, 144
Hillman, Sallie Murfree Frazer, 6, 50, 62, 85
Hillman, Susan, 14, 52
Hillman, Thomas Tennessee (T. T. or Tenny),
    6, 7, 47, 85, 86, 87, 108, 113
Historic Rugby, Inc., 13, 114, 146
Hogan, Kevin, 146
Hollins, Annie, 133, 135
Hollins, Maggie, 135
Hollins, Mrs., 138
Hollins, Porter, 133, 136
Holly, Cass, 42, 91, 146
Homer, Sara Franklin, 113, 145
Hopkinsville, Kentucky, 41, 75
House, Allen Luke Palmer, 77, 78, 105, 108
House, Grace Franklin, 75, 77, 78, 79, 105,
    108, 109, 110, 113, 114
Howard Female College, 104, 105
Howell, Benita (Dr.), 146
Howell, Isabel, 10, 27
Hoyt Family, 79
Hoyt, Lyn Franklin, 92, 141, 145
Humes, Gen., 138
hunting, 22, 48, 51, 71
Huntsville, Alabama, 131
ice-house garden, 34
Immortal Seventy, 8, 9
Indian. *See* Native Americans
Iron and Steel Museum of Alabama, 5, 81
Iron King (referencing Daniel Hillman), 16,
    81, 142
it is more blessed to give than to receive, 63
J. C. & W. H. Wharton (drugstore), 67
Jamestown, Virginia, 5
Jamison, Dr., 134
Jarman, Sara Mac Anderson, 77, 78, 109
Jarman, Walton Maxey, 77, 78, 109
Jasper, Tennessee, 26, 27, 29
Jeffries, L. Q., 137
John Armfield Franklin's will, 120, 125
Johnson, Andrew, 7, 83
just as happy as a big sun-flower, 22
Kelar, A. J. (Col.), 138

Ken Burns' PBS Civil War series, 14
Kenner, F., 138
Kennesaw Mountain, Battle of, 52
Kentucky Insane Asylum, 75, 142
Kentucky Military Institute, 96
Killebrew, J. B. (Col.), 138
Kingstone Lisle, 114
Kirkman, Mary, 133, 138
Kirkpatrick, John Beeman, II, 78, 79, 110
Kirkpatrick, Nan Franklin, 78, 79, 110
Knight, John W., 116
L & N Railroad, 52, 70, 74, 77, 105
Lake Barkley, 89
Land Between the Lakes, 3, 5, 89, 145
Larcomb, Mrs., 136
Lauderdale Family, 8, 90
Lawrence, Mr., 137
Lea, John M. (Judge), 24, 56, 138
Lee, Mrs., 138
Leech, Mrs., 138
Lellyett, T. W., 107
Lindsley, Lit, 133
Lone Pine, 75, 76, 77, 79, 103
Long, Sandra Galbraith, 90, 145
Lord Dunmore's War, 90
Louisiana, 116, 117, 121
Louisville, Kentucky, 8, 12, 40, 70, 76, 96,
    116, 118, 119, 120, 121, 125, 144
Love's Young Dream, 18, 33
Lucindy, 8, 144
Lyon County, Kentucky, 5, 81
Maddin, John W. (Dr.), 63
Maddin, Thomas L. (Dr.), 63
Mammoth Cave, 87
Manly, George (Gen.), 39
Mansker's Station, 90
Maple Summit, 77
Marable Family, 5, 81, 82
Marable Tapestry, 82
Marable, Ann Jones Watson, 5, 81
Marable, Henry Hartwell, 5
Marable, John Hartwell (Dr.), 5, 81, 82
Marine Hospital in Galveston, 15
Marshall, Eugenia, 84
Martin Family, 77, 82, 114
Martin, Allen Palmer House, 77, 78, 79, 103,
    107, 108, 114
Martin, Drew, 110, 114, 146
Martin, Laura Sund, 146
Martin, Luke, 110, 114, 146
Martin, Noel P., 145
Martin, Oscar Eugene, 77, 78, 108
Martin, Patsy, 145

Martin, Terry L., 113, 114
Martin, Thomas D., 83, 145
masquerade ball, 20, 21, 24, 30, 36, 132, 135
Massengale, Katie, 136
Massengale, Ladie, 136
Maury County, Tennessee, 104
Maxwell House Hotel, 53, 83
Mayfield, David, 146
Maywood, 10, 92
McAlister, Maud, 78, 79
McCrea, Bessie, 133, 135, 138
McCrea, Maggie, 133, 135, 138
McFerrin Park, 34, 86
McMackin, T. C. (Gen.), 134, 137, 138
McMinnville, Tennessee, 21, 23, 46, 131, 132, 139
McWhirter, Mrs., 138
Memphis, Tennessee, 77, 135, 137
Methodist Church, 11, 75, 88, 110
mid the falling leaves, as I did 'mid the bloom of May, 65
Mine to the core of my heart..., 70
Mitchellville, Tennessee, 74, 75, 103, 116
Montgomery & Knight, 75, 116, 119
Montgomery County, Tennessee, 13, 81
Moore, Alfred, 136
Moore, M., 134
Morgan and Morgan, 88
Morgan, Judge, 138
Morgan, Mrs. General John Hunt, 16, 138
Morgan's Raiders, 16
Mt. Olivet Cemetery, 77, 79, 83, 86, 87, 90, 105, 106, 113
Mulligan, T. C., 117, 118, 119, 123
Munford, Judge, 115, 119
Murfree Family, 50
Murfree, Elizabeth Maney, 62
Murfree, Fanny Noailles, 50, 84
Murfree, Hardy (Col.), 50, 62
Murfree, Mary Noailles, 50, 84
Murfree, Miss, 50, 133
Murfree, W. J., 138
Murfreesboro, Tennessee, 37, 50, 62, 133
my heart's sweet home, 24
Nash, Mrs., 23
Nashville, 3, 4, 5, 8, 15, 16, 21, 23, 24, 31, 33, 34, 39, 42, 45, 46, 47, 48, 51, 52, 54, 55, 56, 58, 61, 63, 64, 65, 67, 70, 71, 73, 74, 75, 77, 79, 83, 86, 87, 88, 90, 92, 98, 99, 103, 105, 109, 110, 113, 116, 117, 118, 131, 132, 134, 137, 138, 139, 141, 143, 149, 168
Nashville City Hotel, 138

Nashville Commercial Insurance Company, 54
Nashville Female Academy, 12, 97
Nashville Union and American--newspaper, 21, 131, 134, 138, 139, 141, 149
Natchez, Mississippi, 8
Native Americans, 3, 90, 135
New Orleans, Louisiana, 8, 13
Nichol, Mrs., 138
Nicholson House, 137
Nicholson, I. C., Mrs., 137
Noel, Maria Waring, 10
Noel, Silas Mercer (The Rev.), 10, 91, 116, 120
Nora, 42
North Market Street, 74
North Water Avenue, 75
Oakley, 11, 26, 70, 92
O'Bryan, Miss, 138
Oh! Solitude where are the charms that..., 68
Old Hickory Lake, 11, 91
Otey, James Hervey (Bishop), 138, 139
Overton's Hotel, 83
Parker, Beatrice, 57
Partington, Mrs., 133
Patapsco Institute, 12, 97
Paterson, Judith Hillman, 87, 145
Perkins, Miss, 133
Philadelphia, 14, 84, 95
Phillips, Betsy, 146
Phillips, Col., 138
Phrenology, 13
Pilcher, Mrs., 138
Pilot Knob, 8, 52, 79, 90
Pittsburgh, 4, 5, 7, 59, 85
Polk, Leonidas (Bishop and Gen.), 138, 139
Ponce Law, 115, 146
Ponce, Michael, 115, 146
Porter, Alexander James (Capt.), 31, 39, 45, 48, 49, 50, 63, 70, 98, 138
Porter, Annie, 133, 135
Porter, Jimmy, 98
Porter, Mannie, 133, 138
Porter, Martha Watson, 39, 98
Porter, Rebecca Allison, 31, 39, 49, 50, 98
Princeton University, 12
quilt making, 114
Reconstruction era, 37
Reed, Charles, 117, 143
Republican Banner--newspaper, 21, 132
Revolutionary War, 8, 90
Richardson, R. M., 107
Riddle, Genie Borcher, 145

Riverwood Mansion, 39, 98
Roberts, Albert, 138
Robertson, James, 8
Rock City (as Nashville nickname), 42
Rockefeller, John D., 27
Rose Mont, 42
Rothman, Joshua (Professor), 145
Roupes Creek bloomery forge, 81
Rugby, Tennessee, 13, 82, 108, 114, 146
S. M. Scott & Co., 131
Sam Davis Home and Plantation, 5, 146
San Diego, California, 108
Sanderson, John, 10
Saunders, Rolfe S., 138
Saundersville, 8, 51, 52, 70
Scales, David Campbell, 6, 86, 108
Scales, Grace Cora Hillman, 6, 7, 34, 86, 108, 113
Schluter, Miss, 133, 135, 138
Scott, Sam M., 132, 134, 138
Seventh Tennessee Infantry, 12, 96
Sheafe, Charles A. (Capt.), 36, 134, 136
Sheffield-Bradshaw, Ursula, 145
Shelbyville, Kentucky, 33, 34, 36, 39
Shiloh, Battle of, 37
slaves and slavery, 3, 4, 8, 11, 26, 38, 46, 81, 88, 90, 91, 93, 99, 117, 140, 141, 142, 143, 144
Smith, A. (Gen.), 138
Smyrna, Tennessee, 5
Sneed, Susan Hofsass, 146
Snow, Susan, 31, 146
Social Circle, Georgia, 68
South Pittsburg, Tennessee, 27
South Water Street, 42
Southern Methodist Publishing House, 88
Spring Haven Mansion (Hard Times), 11, 93, 146
stand not upon the order, 47
Station Camp Creek, 8, 90
stereopticon, 31
still small voice, 21
Stoneridge Farms, 99
Stones River, Battle of, 37
Strickland, William, 92
Sumner County, 3, 4, 5, 8, 10, 12, 42, 70, 74, 79, 93, 110, 111, 115, 117, 118, 123, 125, 131, 137, 139, 143, 145
Sumner County Archives, 76, 115, 146
Sumner County Circuit Court, 118, 121
Sumner County Convention and Visitor's Bureau, 10, 91
Sumner County Historical Society, 115, 145

Sumner County Museum, 10
Sumner, Col., 138
Sunset Rock, 44
Tallahassee, Florida, 67, 96, 116, 118, 119, 120, 121
Tammany Wood, 98
Tannehill Iron Works, 5
Tannehill Ironworks Historical State Park, 81
Tennessee Iron Store, 54, 74
Tennessee Rolling Works, 54, 89
Tennessee School for the Blind, 24
Tennessee State Library and Archives, 46, 146
Tennessee Stave Factory, 21, 27
Tennessee Supreme Court, 76, 115, 118, 119, 120, 121, 122, 126
Terzian, Grace Paine, 81, 145
The Daily American--newspaper, 99, 115, 118, 119
Third National Bank, 54
Thirteenth Virginia Calvary, 12, 96
Thomas Hughes Free Public Library, 13
Thomas, Aaron, 81, 146
Thomas, Annie, 135
Thomas, Miss, 133
Thomas, Mrs., 138
Thomson, Kenneth, 74, 76, 115, 145
Tracey City, Tennessee, 139
Transylvania Medical University, 91
Trigg County, Kentucky, 5, 23, 41, 81, 89
Trigg Furnace, 87, 89
Trousdale-Baskerville House, 10, 92
Tullahoma, Tennessee, 131
Turner Cottage, 34
Turner, James J., 117, 118, 119, 124
Turney, John E., 107
Typhoid, 77, 108
Ullrich, Danielle, 146
University of Alabama, 145
University of Nashville, 55
University of Pennsylvania, 15, 95
University of Tennessee, 84, 146
University of the South, 93, 131
Van Bibber, Adele Franklin, 9, 10, 12, 15, 17, 20, 21, 22, 23, 30, 34, 38, 47, 91, 94, 97, 116, 118, 121, 124, 125, 139
Van Bibber, George Lindenberger, 9, 12, 15, 17, 23, 40, 46, 54, 97, 116, 121, 139
Van Buren, Martin, 82
vanished like a dream, 21
Volunteer State Community College, 11
Washington, Georgia, 69, 116
Watson Family, 82

Waugh, Samuel Bell, 15, 83
Waverly Church of Christ, 98
Waverly, Tennessee, 98
We parted by the mountainside..., 22
Webb School, 77, 105
Westcott, Charles, 84
Westcott, Mary, 84
Wharton, J. C., 53, 67
Wharton, Mrs., 53
Wharton, W. H., 53, 67
Whitney, W. T. (Tom), 145
Williams, Harry, 146
Williams, Nannie Haskins, 14
Williams, Peg, 146
Williams, Rodney, 146

Wilson Farm, 10
Wilson, B. F. (Col.), 138
Wilson, Mr., 134, 136
Wilson, S. F., 117, 118, 119, 124
Winston, Eliza, 133, 135, 138
Winston, J. D. (Dr.), 24, 30, 57, 131
Winston, Jennie, 20, 24, 30, 57, 59, 133, 135, 138
Winston, Lula, 135, 138
Woods, Georgia, 133, 138
Woods, Mary, 133, 138
World War I, 106
Wynnewood State Historic Site, 114, 146
Yerger Family, 30
Yerger, William (Judge), 31, 138

www.ingramcontent.com/pod-product-compliance
Lightning Source LLC
Chambersburg PA
CBHW052031070526
44584CB00016B/1993